ALL THESE THINGS THAT I'VE DONE

MY INSANE, IMPROBABLE ROCK LIFE

Matt Pinfield

with Mitchell Cohen

SCRIBNER

New York   London   Toronto   Sydney   New Delhi

SCRIBNER
An Imprint of Simon & Schuster, Inc.
1230 Avenue of the Americas
New York, NY 10020

First Scribner hardcover edition September 2016

SCRIBNER and design are registered trademarks of The Gale Group, Inc.,
used under license by Simon & Schuster, Inc., the publisher of this work.

For information about special discounts for bulk purchases,
please contact Simon & Schuster Special Sales at 1-866-506-1949
or business@simonandschuster.com.

The Simon & Schuster Speakers Bureau can bring authors to
your live event. For more information or to book an event, contact the
Simon & Schuster Speakers Bureau at 1-866-248-3049
or visit our website at www.simonspeakers.com.

Interior design by Kyle Kabel

Manufactured in the United States of America

3   5   7   9   10   8   6   4   2

Library of Congress Cataloging-in-Publication Data is available.

ISBN 978-1-4767-9389-4
ISBN 978-1-4767-9392-4 (ebook)

This book is dedicated to my amazing mother,
Nancy Helena Pinfield,
and my late, great father, George William Pinfield,
for their undying support throughout my life

To my beautiful daughters,
Jessica Lynn and Maya Penelope

My sister, Colleen, Timmy, and Devin O'Neill

My brother, Glenn, Laura, and Benjamin Pinfield

And special thanks to my cowriter, Mitchell Cohen;
Laura Nolan; Danny Goldberg; and John Glynn
for making this book a reality

Contents

Introduction

Paul McCartney and me

My relationship with Paul McCartney's voice is longer than with anyone else's except the people in my immediate family. That's a simple fact. One of my earliest memories is from when I was three years old, sitting on the floor with a record player. I'd say, "Beatles! Beatles! Give me Beatles!" and my brother and sister would put on the Capitol 45 of "A Hard Day's Night" and then the other side, "I Should Have Known Better," and I would rock back and forth to the music. Like every kid, I suppose, I thought that they were singing to me personally, and the sound took hold of me. That's how all this got started, and if my reading and motor skills had been more developed, it would have been my entry into the life of a DJ. As it was, I needed my family to be my audio engineers.

Not long ago, I had the chance to sit down for an extended interview with Sir Paul and ask him the questions I'd stored up for decades. I wanted to know everything: the real story behind the Beatles' *Yesterday and Today* "Butcher" cover, what it was like when a knife was held to his throat in Nigeria when Wings were recording *Band on the Run*, how "Drive My Car" was written. I had to hear from him what it was like to play "Back in the U.S.S.R." in Red Square, what the lyrics of "Jet" meant, and the events that led up to his writing one of the most rocking James Bond themes ever, "Live and Let Die." He told me how "New," the title song from his current album, the one we were doing the session to promote, was written on his dad's piano, which was purchased at the music store owned by Brian Epstein's father. I had what amounted to a lifetime of questions, and a limited window to ask them all. Even I can't talk that fast.

At the end of our conversation, Paul said that if he didn't have anniversary plans with his wife, he and I could head down to a pub and continue to talk. Moments like that still seem surreal to me. Let's face it, without the Beatles, who basically invented rock culture, I probably never would have thought about making a spot for myself in the music world. I remember as a kid listening to *Rubber Soul* in my basement and thinking how brilliant, creative, fertile, and non-sanctioned it sounded, how empowering it was. The Beatles changed the world because they made kids like me feel as though they could do anything.

So you can imagine what it means to be face to face with McCartney, and to not only tell him what he meant to me personally but to be the surrogate for all those fans as impassioned as I am. My job is to ask the questions that those other fans would ask if they had the chance, and I take my job seriously.

No matter how many encounters I've had like that over the past thirty-plus years—it has to be into the thousands at this point—I always confront a duality. I'm extracting the inside stories on behalf of the audience that isn't in the room, but I'm also approaching the encounter as a fan who can't quite believe he's having the experience. When it's someone like Sir Paul, or the Rolling Stones or Jimmy Page and Robert Plant, I'm with musicians who existed on another plane entirely for me; they were unreachable, unknowable figures from a place distant and remote, sending me messages through their songs that I spent hours, days, trying to decipher. They were voices on vinyl when I was at my most impressionable.

And there are other musicians, like Elvis Costello and Paul Weller, closer to my generation, but no less figures I admired from afar. It's jarring at first when our off-mic discussions become intimate. When I was a teenager, I was just one of the crowd—watching Elvis Costello and the Attractions in the Princeton gym in April 1979, or the Jam at the Palladium in New York City that same eventful month. How could I ever have conceived of a scenario where Elvis and I would be sharing thoughts about aging and mortality, about his ailing father and my brother's struggle with Parkinson's? Or where Paul and I would commiserate over the agony of divorce? These guys, through their music, guided me through every emotional challenge, and then years later, those barriers have fallen and we're just men at a similar stage in life. I think about Joey and Lou and Layne and Scott and David and all the other flawed fallen heroes and friends, and I realize how fortunate I've been to have had those moments in public and private, to still be here when there were times when my survival was by no means a safe bet.

I'll tell you, sometimes I've broken down in tears contemplating it, the sheer improbability of my journey, because there are so many people like me.

There are guys like me everywhere—record fairs, used LP stores, on the internet arguing the relative merits of the Alarm and Big Country—but I'm the one who sounds like a bullfrog with bronchitis and looks like Uncle Fester, if the Addams Family were a late-'70s punk band. There are so many times over the years when I've asked myself, "How the fuck did I get here?" How did I become that guy who broke past all the security guards, all the obstacles, to have these incredible adventures doing what I love the most? Fans approach me all the time. "What was Kurt Cobain like?" "Did you really party with Axl and Slash?" And sometimes they just say, "Man, you are one lucky dude."

The dream of access, of proximity, began when I was a kid sitting in front of my record player. It was never enough to just listen to an album or see a concert. I wanted to *know*. This is my version of a *Greatest Hits (Volume One)* album, and each chapter is a rock song. Some are epic and span decades— my longtime connections to artists like U2 and Bowie—and some are shorter, like those great early singles by the Beatles that summed up everything they needed to say in 150 exhilarating seconds. I want it to have the power of a Led Zeppelin album, the vivid highs and thrills of a Springsteen album, the sense of new possibilities of Nirvana's *Nevermind*, and the bracing candor of a Bowie album. I want you to be there, in the moment, taking the ride with me.

Dropping the Needle:
Side One, Track One

The label was black and off-white. The two eight-pointed stars at the top were gold, and so was the logo of the record company: *wand*, with a lowercase *w*. Except for the address (1650 Broadway, New York, N.Y.), the rest of the information was stamped in red: "TWIST AND SHOUT" (PHIL MEDLEY–BERT RUSSELL) THE ISLEY BROTHERS. The flip side was "Spanish Twist." I was three years old, and my mother and I were in a five-and-dime store in Dunellen, New Jersey, where they sold cutout, slightly dated 45 rpm singles. She knew I already loved music so she would let me pick them out, even though I couldn't read and was making my musical selections based on whether the label looked interesting. I remember walking into the drugstore and looking at records we couldn't afford, and then going to the five-and-dime where you could buy three singles for fifteen cents.

I already knew what I liked and what I didn't. My parents bought me children's records on the Disneyland or Peter Pan kids' labels, and I threw them under the refrigerator.

"What happened to those records?" my mom would ask.

Until the day we moved, they never knew. I hid them,

because the only music I wanted to listen to was the music my older siblings, Glenn and Colleen, brought home. By 1964, I knew the difference between the Peter Pan records and the Beatles. It was obvious. We had one of those record players where you could stack a bunch of 45s and when one was over, the next one would drop and play. Mostly, we kids had singles, but I was fascinated by a couple of full albums that were part of our small collection: the soundtrack to *A Hard Day's Night, Elvis' Golden Records*, with all his early hits: "Don't Be Cruel," "Heartbreak Hotel," "Jailhouse Rock." At the time I had no idea what the artists were singing about or what the songs meant. I was responding to the sound, the plunk of the record dropping on the player, the hiss of the needle before it finds the groove, the rolling drums and ecstatic harmonies that start off "She Loves You." It was the most exciting thing in the world to me.

My mom says I was always either sitting in front of the TV watching *My Favorite Martian* or in front of the record player drawing on the single picture sleeves. I had a very visual memory, so I would know by what was on the cover, or on the label, which song was on the record. I learned how to place the records on the spindle, how to use the tone arm. I was already my own private DJ, with one turntable, no microphone, a pile of mono 45s on the floor.

Music was always in my house. My mother played piano. My dad liked to sing "Ebb Tide," and for a time was a background singer for Frankie Laine. He was also a Korean War veteran, an officer in the marines. They gave him amphetamines to stay awake during night duty, and his heart couldn't take it. He had a heart attack, got an honorable discharge, and had to start his life over. After he came back from Korea and found out that the woman he had been planning to propose to was seeing someone else, he threw the engagement ring in the river and reconnected with my mom, who was already divorced and raising my brother, Glenn, who's ten years older than I am. Glenn was the coolest big brother ever, a real anti-establishment guy through the '60s. He was at Woodstock, and at Altamont.

My dad went back to school at the University of Georgia and sent letters to my mom, whom he'd met when they were both just fourteen. Recently, my eldest daughter found a letter that my mother had sent to her mother. It read, "Oh! This George Pinfield is being very persistent. I don't think I'm going to get involved with him."

My dad was, as the letter said, persistent (that's a trait I got from him), and my mother allowed herself to be wooed down to Albany, Georgia. They got married and had my sister, then moved to Athens. My mother worked at Benson's Fruitcake Factory. I came along six years later, very unexpectedly, and the family moved to New Jersey, to a small town called Dunellen, in Middlesex County. Maybe six thousand people, none of them famous except for one guy, Tom Scharpling, who would later write for the TV show *Monk* and host a comedy show on WFMU.

We three kids loved music, and my mom and dad had decided it was worth fifteen bucks to buy a used 45 record player from a neighbor, and a box of records. It's weird to say that I found my calling by the time I was in kindergarten, but there's no other way to put it. All I wanted to do was listen to records and get other people as excited about them as I was. I have a vivid memory of being five years old, in 1966, and being in a hot car with my dad (nobody I knew had air-conditioning then). I heard all those sun-and-summer songs: "Sunshine Superman" by Donovan, "Sunny

Afternoon" by the Kinks, "Sunny" by Bobby Hebb, "Summer in the City" by the Lovin' Spoonful. I went to kindergarten clutching my Mercury 45 of the Blues Magoos doing "(We Ain't Got) Nothin' Yet," and someone sat on it on the school bus. It broke, and I cried. I was going to play the record during show-and-tell. That was already my thing: I'd brought in "Snoopy vs. the Red Baron" by the Royal Guardsmen, and "Along Comes Mary" by the Association. I was the Music Guy, the DJ, the Authority. At the age of five I had my whole adult identity already in place.

That same year, I made my television debut. Every day I watched a children's show called *Birthday House*, hosted by Paul Tripp, on channel 4 in New York. You could be in the studio audience only if it was on or around your birthday. My mother wrote a letter to WNBC to get me on for my fifth birthday, and that was the first time I visited Manhattan. All of us went—my parents, brother, and sister. I was wearing a little striped suit. The show gave me a king's crown and a snare drum and a bag of goodies. I have a still photo from that day, but no footage. Years later I tried to track down a copy of the kinescope and found out that they'd all been erased or discarded. There were even *Birthday House* records; I've seen an LP on Musicor Records that has the song "Hi Mike" that Tripp sang while we kids all marched around in the studio. Another song on the record was "Everybody Up." Even at five, I thought those songs were too childish. I was way past "If You Just Make Believe." I was already listening to the Stones' "19th Nervous Breakdown."

I have a report card from this time that says, "Matt gets straight A's but we need to keep him busy. He gets bored very easily." The only thing that kept me focused was music. No one called it ADD in the mid-'60s, but that's exactly what I had. If I could control the classroom's record player, if I could spin Beatles and Monkees records and talk about what was special about them, I could imagine that I was like the New York disc jockeys at WABC, WINS, and WMCA: Cousin Bruce Morrow, Dan Ingram, Murray the K, Harry Harrison.

I remember nearly every song, every LP cut and 45, that came out in the summer of 1966: *Revolver* and *Pet Sounds*, *Sunshine Superman* by Donovan and *(Turn On) the Music Machine*. "Psychotic Reaction" by the Count Five. It was perfect that Glenn was a decade older than me, because garage rock was made for fifteen-year-old boys, all the pent-up sexual energy, the aggression and confusion. Glenn was the ideal garage-rock demographic, and he in turn gave it to me. I didn't understand the sex or the angst, but I fell deeply in love with the sound.

We didn't have much furniture, so I'd roam around the living room, taking a fan and singing into it like a microphone. (All my "scientific" experiments had to relate to music in some way. At a science fair in fifth or sixth grade, my project involved an oscillator and the sound waves created by Alice Cooper and Sly and the Family Stone records.)

It's crazy what sticks with me, and how almost all of it relates to music. My dad was always creative and resourceful. When we moved from Dunellen to East Brunswick, he built us an aboveground pool. Since the mere idea of being outdoors without a soundtrack was unthinkable, I brought the record player to the backyard. The pool was only four or five feet deep, but I was told not to go in without a life preserver. One day during a family barbecue I climbed up the ladder, jumped in, and sank to the bottom.

I'd left the Cyrkle's "Red Rubber Ball" on the record player. I remember this. I have a blurry vision of being underwater, at the bottom of the pool, and the sight of the bubbles, and my neighbor David diving in to rescue me. He saved my life, and after I was yelled at, and punished, I put "Red Rubber Ball" back on and played it again. That's how my fucking brain works: I can be drowning, and still know what song is playing.

I can still remember one of my earliest nightmares. In it, people I knew were shrunk down to the size of ants and came out of the ground pointing guns at me. For the entire dream, I was hearing the Kinks' "I'm Not Like Everybody Else." I always played the B-sides of every single, and often I found I was drawn to them more than to the hits: I felt like I was paying attention to something most people ignored. When I flipped over "Sunny Afternoon" and discovered "I'm Not Like Everybody Else," I was shocked by how raw and naked it was. It sounded defiant, but also kind of wounded. It was a statement of individuality. Ray Davies was speaking directly to me, and to kids like me, but you had to turn the record over to hear him. That's a rule of mine: *Turn the record over*, find out what's on the other side. Although the message of "Sunny Afternoon" was pretty dispirited, it sounded, well, sunny. "I'm Not Like Everybody Else" didn't. It was a cry from the soul, and I related to it, and it haunted me in my dreams.

Because that's how I felt: different and isolated. I know a lot of serious rock fans feel this way, because they tell me so. They call me, e-mail me, and let me know that for them there's nothing casual about being a music fan. For most people, music is only one diverting component of their lives. It's amusement. Songs come and go. They listen to whatever's on the radio, whatever they feel like streaming. They hear music in clubs when they're out drinking and trying to get laid. It's in the background.

It was *never* like that for me.

I wasn't super lonely. I had friends, but they didn't have the same passion for the music that I did, so it was a beautiful but isolating experience. Music was my dreamland. I'd listen to a song and imagine myself into it, not even knowing what "Sunny Afternoon" meant, or even half the lyrics of "Summer in the City." It just hit me on an almost subliminal level, the emotional power.

Before I had any idea about heartbreak, what it really meant, I was that kid who cried over records. Even though I hadn't experienced love, and didn't know what to do with a girl if I liked her, the power of music made me feel as though I understood it. The next year, when I was infatuated with a different girl, Susan, I played the Buckinghams' 45 of "Susan" over and over. I'm sure this is not normal for a seven year old.

By 1967, rock had become an obsession. I was immersed. I'd sneak into my brother's and sister's bedrooms, pulling out their records and playing them: *Disraeli Gears, Are You Experienced?* My sister was in love with Jim Morrison, and that's how I discovered the Doors; she had a life-size poster of Morrison in tight leather pants taped to the back of her bedroom door. She was fifteen, and Morrison got her hormones racing, and she listened to that first album, the one with "Break on Through" and "Light My Fire," constantly.

When my brother met his first wife, she had been a big Beatles and British Invasion fan, and she had a collection of 45s that she gave me. Thanks to the rapid succession of singles in that Top 40 era, the haul included like 150 discs. So I was listening to records like the Zombies' "Tell Her No" along with current hits like Buffalo Springfield's "For What It's Worth" (and the B-side, of course, "Do I Have to Come Right Out and Say It"). I'd loved those songs when they were on the radio, but now I could sit in front of the record player and analyze Buffalo Springfield, analyze the Zombies. I had inherited a goldmine.

My sister-in-law was an early fan of mine. When my parents would worry about my being hyper-crazy about the music, she was the one who would tell them, "Matt is going to be all right." She was like the older sister played by Zooey Deschanel in *Almost Famous*. She assured me that someday I was going to be cool.

I was truly obsessed. I always had the transistor radio on as I did my homework. At night I kept it under my pillow, with the one tiny headphone. I hated Sunday nights, because WINS, WABC, and WMCA would do all their shitty public-affairs programming, and I was like, "Where did the music go?" I was pissed off. Or I would wake up on Sunday mornings and there'd be some religious programming. Fuck that. Where are my songs? Anything that didn't relate to rock 'n' roll I could give a shit about. Later, girls and getting high were my other main pursuits, but even they never bumped music from being number one.

I needed to acquire more and more records and found ways to do it on a minimal budget. A nearby department store had a big bin of prewrapped 45s, ten singles for two dollars. You could only see the names of the two records on the outside. Maybe they were familiar, maybe they weren't. The other eight singles were hidden by the plastic wrap.

Most of those hidden songs never got played on the radio. That didn't matter to me; it was just a two-dollar investment, and one of my favorite tracks came from those hidden 45s: "Six O'Clock" by the Lovin' Spoonful, which I still love to this day. In another batch I got a Mustang Records single from the Bobby Fuller Four, a cover of Buddy Holly's "Love's Made a Fool of You" backed with "Don't Ever Let Me Know." I really liked both sides, so that was a bargain right there. Of course sometimes the middle records would be crappy shit like Ronnie Dove. I had to suck it up.

It's an impressionable time, at eight, nine, ten years old, being stirred by something we can connect to. At first we're probably drawn to the melody, the way choruses repeat and return, and then we look for something in the lyric, something to access the world the words are creating. I was that age when rock stars started to die off: Jimi Hendrix, Janis Joplin, Brian Jones of the Rolling Stones. I knew they had died from drugs and that scared the shit out of me. I would eventually become an alcoholic and a drug addict myself, and I guess any shrink would say that the reason drugs frightened me so much was because they fascinated me. As much as I loved positive, uplifting music, groups like the Lovin' Spoonful and the Byrds, I also gravitated toward music that frightened me, like the way dark, violent movies give you a rush. Drugs were like that too.

When I was ten I discovered my sister or brother's copy of the third Velvet Underground album, the one with "What Goes On," "Beginning to See the Light," "Candy Says," and "After Hours." It freaked me out. The band looked so strange on the cover. Lou Reed was relatively clean-cut and preppy, but he's the only band member looking into the camera. On the back, he's sliced in half, holding a cigarette. Who were these dangerous-looking people? I didn't know a single thing about them or the whole Plastic Inevitable scene, or Warhol or photographer Billy Name, who took that eerie cover shot. I didn't know "Candy Says" was about Warhol superstar Candy Darling. I had no sociological context. It was all about the music and the mystique. I was absorbing it all on a song-by-song basis. "Pale Blue Eyes" didn't resonate with me because it was so slow and melancholy, but tracks like "What Goes On" hooked me instantly.

I thought the Steppenwolf song "Don't Step on the Grass, Sam" was pretty dangerous. I remember that in the late '60s there were public service films warning kids about marijuana and harder drugs. Because my dad was the AV department head, he could—or let's say *would*, because I have no idea whether he had permission or not—bring home the school's movie projector and we'd watch movies on our wall, things he'd take out of those old metal canisters, like Flash Gordon serials and those cautionary scare flicks about how dangerous drugs were. They creeped me out, because I was already into psychedelic bands like Big Brother and the Holding Company and Hendrix. I had *Cheap Thrills* and *Axis: Bold as Love*, which is still my favorite Hendrix album. Their drug-related deaths frightened me, and so did these crappy little movies.

My brother, as I said, was really political, and I remember the fights around the dinner table about Vietnam. Glenn was so antiwar, and my dad was a Korean War vet with a temper, and the fights—most of the time verbal, occasionally physical—were agonizing for me. The turmoil that was going on in my own house was something else I needed to escape through music. But Glenn looked out for me. When I was around ten years old, he bought me John Lennon's *Plastic Ono Band* album, the Grateful Dead's *American Beauty*, and the first Led Zeppelin album. That's how my brain is wired; I couldn't tell you very many details from my childhood that aren't in some way associated with what records were involved. Through all the haze of my craziness, all the memories that have been suppressed or burnt away, there isn't a song that hasn't stuck with me. That was my drug before drugs became my drug. I'd listen to every album in the house at least once: my parents' albums by Al Hirt (he looked like he was about 106 years old, God bless him) or Dionne Warwick. I just thought Hirt was weird—like, why do my mother and father like this?—but I had to put every record on at least once. I'm sorry, but I think I threw Mr. Hirt's album into the garbage. Now I might be able to put him into context, the New Orleans jazz tradition and all that, and the fact that his hit record "Java" was an Allen Toussaint song. But back then, he was just a bearded fat guy with a trumpet. I had my own musical criteria, even at ten. I was open-minded enough to give every piece of vinyl a shot, but just as quick to rip the needle off the platter and fling the damn thing into the trash.

People take for granted now that they can take their music library with them. But back in those days, you had to be innovative. I never wanted to be separated from my music, so I had this shitty mono General Electric cassette recorder, and I held the microphone next to the speaker to tape all of *Cosmo's Factory* by Creedence Clearwater Revival, right off the vinyl. Then I would find a way to wrap the cassette player to the front of my bicycle and blast Creedence while I rode around the neighborhood. Already I was trying to invent a portable player to carry my own music around. Now I walk around with twenty thousand songs in my pocket.

I also wanted a real stereo, but they were expensive, so my dad decided he was going to build me one from scratch. He was brilliant, a physics teacher. He ordered the knobs, all the wiring, the transistors. He had separate tone and volume knobs, and a separate system for each channel, so the thing was a big square box. He bought the wood and shellacked it, bought the pieces for the turntable from a component catalog, and sat the turntable in the case. He built the speakers by hand. My dad knew that my dream was about music and wouldn't let our modest financial circumstances be an obstacle. He thought of ways to make it happen for me.

And my dad kicked off my broadcasting career—well, it wasn't that "broad," actually—when he built me a low-frequency AM transmitter, then wired it up to the TV antenna on our roof. I had the power to be a *very* local DJ (like three blocks). I called my station WBBB (I couldn't think of anything more catchy; maybe it should have been WMAT?) and made my friends DJs and gave them fake names, and every neighborhood kid could hear us if they tuned their portable radios to 1680 on the AM dial, as far to the right as you can get and still receive any signal at all. We had two turntables—Radio Shack made the cheapest we could find—and my dad brought home old mics they were throwing out at his school. On Saturdays I'd play the whole Free *Fire and Water* album, or all of *Quadrophenia*.

It was dream time. When I wasn't doing my own shows, I was listening to the radio. There was one DJ, Rich Phoenix— what a great radio name, and it wasn't made-up—who befriended me when I was around ten or eleven. He was on WCTC, 1450 on the dial in New Brunswick, and had the night shift. I'd call him up and bug him. I was just this talkative kid. I'd ask him about songs and records, and he was cool to me. He made me listen to Buddy Holly: he recorded a few Holly songs for me on a reel-to-reel player and they sounded better than any of my vinyl records. It was like Buddy Holly was in the room with me.

Rich Phoenix was an inspiration. He let me come to the studio, and even showed me how to work the equipment. My parents would drive me to the station and then pick me up after Rich's shift. I learned how to cue up a record, how to transition in and out of songs. I knew it was what I wanted to do.

There's beauty in having the platform to tell people about music that you love. You're a messenger; you're turning people on to things they wouldn't have heard otherwise. I wanted people to appreciate the songs the way I did, whether they interpreted them the same way or not. You're giving people context and framework. You're constructing a narrative.

*   *   *

I'd sit in Rich's studio and watch how he placed the vinyl on the turntable, and to this day, when I see a movie that's set in the '50s, '60s, or '70s, and it shows a vinyl record spinning, that's still a very romantic notion to me. It can't be replicated with a CD or an audio file. You can't see the label or the grooves, the spot where the needle meets the record. There's no mechanical ambience. No weight. No visual personality.

We're all outsiders, a tribe linked by our single-minded passion. At some early point in our lives, everything changed the minute we heard a song on the radio, or the night someone played us a record, or we flipped on the television set and saw a band—the Beatles, or Nirvana—take three minutes to completely transform the world. It doesn't matter how we got there, or what the catalyst was; in that moment, everything reversed and started pointing in a different direction. Sometimes it was faint: a radio station tuned in from a distance, a small article in a UK music magazine, an import single we had to hunt for, an oldie that had escaped us the first time around only to become a total obsession. Sometimes we thought we were alone, that no one else was experiencing this. We listened in darkened rooms to the drop of the needle on the vinyl and the yowl that followed: the Velvet Underground, the Ramones, Eddie Cochran, the Pretty Things, Suicide, the sounds of defiance and danger that we were drawn to. We felt isolated but yearned for connection.

*   *   *

Musicians had to compress everything they needed to say into around 165 seconds. Maybe as much as 250, but not much more. The greatness of rock is that it rewards those of us with short attention spans. That's how it can get its (literal) hooks into us when we're kids.

So that's how it started for me, before I knew almost anything else, before I was aware of my brain, my body, the outside world, anything beyond my room and my family, I went where the music took me. You don't start off by thinking about it as a lifelong journey. You really don't think at all. You simply respond.

50 ESSENTIAL ROCK ALBUMS:
THE '60s

The Band

The Beach Boys—*Pet Sounds*

The Beatles—*Rubber Soul*

The Beatles—*The White Album*

Buffalo Springfield 1

Byrds—*Younger Than Yesterday*

Chicago—*Chicago Transit Authority*

Cream—*Disraeli Gears*

Creedence Clearwater Revival—*Green River*

Crosby, Stills and Nash

The Dave Clark 5—*Greatest Hits*

Donovan's Greatest Hits

The Doors—*Strange Days*

Bob Dylan—*Blonde on Blonde*

The Hollies—*Greatest Hits*

Jeff Beck Group—*Truth*

Jefferson Airplane—*Surrealistic Pillow*

The Jimi Hendrix Experience—*Axis: Bold As Love*

The Kinks—*Face to Face*

Led Zeppelin

Led Zeppelin II

Love—*Forever Changes*

The Lovin' Spoonful—*Hums of the Lovin' Spoonful*

MC5—*Kick Out the Jams*

Moby Grape

The Monkees—*Headquarters*

The Music Machine—*(Turn On) The Music Machine*

Pink Floyd—*The Piper at the Gates of Dawn*

The Rascals—*Time Peace*

Otis Redding—*The History of Otis Redding*

Quicksilver Messenger Service

The Rolling Stones—*Through The Past, Darkly
(Big Hits, Vol. 2)*

The Rolling Stones—*Beggars Banquet*

Simon and Garfunkel—*Bookends*

Sly and the Family Stone—*Stand!*

Small Faces—*Ogdens' Nut Gone Flake*

Steppenwolf—*The Second*

The Stooges 1

Ten Years After—*Ssssh*

Traffic

Scott Walker—*Scott 3*

Vanilla Fudge

The Velvet Underground—*The Velvet Underground & Nico*

The Velvet Underground

The Who—*The Who Sell Out*

The Who—*Meaty Beaty Big and Bouncy*

Yardbirds—*Having a Rave up with the Yardbirds*

Neil Young—*Everybody Knows This Is Nowhere*

Zombies—*Odessey and Oracle*

Nuggets: Original Artyfacts from the First Psychedelic Era

Metal Gurus
and Other Discoveries

Early days of my Bowie fandom

A four-LP compilation album came out when I was twelve, *Superstars of the 70's*. As its title implies, it was an eclectic hodgepodge of music across the rock and pop spectrum, kind of what the *Now That's What I Call Music* series is: a crash course in What's Happening. One of my neighbors bought it off a TV ad, and I borrowed it. Come to think of it, I probably never gave it back. You wouldn't think a slapped-together collection of random tracks could be so influential, but to me it was like opening a treasure chest. I played that album constantly; it had the Stones, Hendrix, the Dead, the Allman Brothers, and Faces; soul music (Aretha, Otis) and folkie stuff (Judy Collins, Arlo Guthrie); prog-rock (Yes, ELP) and pop (the Bee Gees, the Beach Boys). I studied it all, every single cut on all eight sides. That was where I discovered Black Sabbath's "Paranoid" and James Taylor's "Fire and Rain." It was like my encyclopedia. It had cool oddities like Jo Jo Gunne's "Run Run Run" and "Hush" by Deep Purple.

You can begin with "Hush" and Blue Cheer's "Summertime Blues" and trace their skid marks to Iron Butterfly, Grand Funk, and Spinal Tap and all the way to Korn and Slipknot. Throw in "Born to Be Wild" by Steppenwolf (with the line "I like smoke and lightning / Heavy metal thunder"), also from '68, and you have the ABC of metal. I didn't quite get Deep Purple off the bat (all three of their first singles were covers), and Sabbath was one of the bands that I may have been too young to grasp (confession: I was frightened of them), but on those four LPs, there was so much to explore. I will never forget how Alice Cooper's "School's Out" kicked it off, and then how the mood abruptly changed with Seals and Crofts' "Summer Breeze": this album was programmed, apparently, by a primitive form of the iPod shuffle setting.

I remember those albums so vividly and the impression they made on me. People might not imagine me as a "Seals and Crofts guy," but at that age, I found something to latch on to in almost every song, even if it was only the sound of the guitar on "Summer Breeze." It's all a matter of when songs come into your life. Decades later, I was in New Orleans with a British A&R guy, and a super cute girl came up to me in a bar on Bourbon Street. We started making out, and when we were dancing, Seals and Crofts came on the jukebox, and I instantly flashed back to that collection. Those things imprint on you.

Stephen Stills's "Love the One You're With" is on that compilation, and my dick got hard. It's not the sexiest record in the world, but the idea of grabbing the girl closest to you and touching her, it got me aroused. Hey, you can't control that, especially not at twelve, so thanks, Stephen. As random as those discs are, if you play me any cut I can still tell you what the tracks are right before or after it. The last songs on side one of the third disc were Jackson Browne's "Doctor My Eyes" and Black Sabbath's "Paranoid," two songs that you'd never otherwise think of in succession.

I may not have known what the word *paranoid* meant, but I did look it up, and I knew I had to get the *Paranoid* album. It'd been out a while by then, but how would I ever have known about it? No one was playing "War Pigs" on the radio. What was this? "Rat Salad," "Electric Funeral," "Hand of Doom," "Iron Man" . . . the guy with the shield and blurry sword on the cover. Back then there was no parental screening process, no WARNING: EXPLICIT LYRICS stamped across album covers. Thank God. I'd bring edgy albums into the house and play them in private listening ceremonies. It was like sneaking into an adults-only movie, or finding an issue of *Penthouse*, the thrill of the illicit.

There weren't as many musical subcultures then. I was drawn to what you might consider protometal, records with loud, crunching guitars and vocals straining to be heard above the din, but it wasn't like I would have called myself a metal kid, as much as I was drawn to the angst and the energy. I was a big fan of rock with riffs, and at the same time I loved the Dead's *American Beauty* but wasn't a mini-Deadhead. There wasn't that much of a division between the metal kids and the hippie kids. The kids who listened to the Dead also listened to Led Zeppelin and Black

Sabbath, the same way free-form FM radio would play "In-A-Gadda-Da-Vida" and maybe a Marvin Gaye track or the debut album by Chicago (back when they were still called Chicago Transit Authority). I never self-identified with a single genre, I was just a musical sponge. I'd go over to a friend's house, and it wouldn't matter if he had a Ping-Pong table or a pool table, if we were playing Rock 'Em Sock 'Em Robots or Battling Tops, what I cared about was what music was playing. The activity was the backdrop, music was in the foreground. I'd bring over my own records, and raid their collections.

With these early metal antecedents, there was an element of, This is too weird for my parents, too weird for Top 40 radio, too angry, too aggressive—and that was why I liked it. It was trickier for me to get into Sabbath than it had been with Led Zeppelin, because at least Led Zeppelin was more blues and rock. It wasn't that far from the Stones and the Yardbirds; Sabbath moved the needle further into the red. "Paranoid" is to me one of the greatest songs ever recorded, and it was almost an afterthought. It has the brevity of a single—it's under three minutes—so you almost don't have the time to absorb it. It crashes into you and speeds off like a musical hit-and-run.

The other side of the disc featured the Allman Brothers Band, Faces, and Graham Nash's "Chicago," about the riots during the summer of '68 Democratic Convention that my brother had gone to, the one where the cops and protesters clashed, and activists like Abbie Hoffman and Jerry Rubin were arrested. And Keith Richards singing lead with the Stones on a cut from *Exile on Main Street*. It all makes no sense, there's no continuity, but the sequence works the way my musical brain works, and I already know I want to play records for people and this is how I'd do it, skipping around from here to there.

It was a blast to be a preteen at the start of the '70s. George Lucas's *American Graffiti*, an affectionate flashback to one summer night in 1962, with wall-to-wall oldies, came out in '73, in the midst of a revival of interest in the music of the '50s and the pre-Beatles part of the '60s. *Rock Is Here to Stay* was another four-LP (for $6.99) compilation I bought, via a company called Dynamic House. I got the money together and gave it to my parents, who wrote a check and mailed it in, and then every day for weeks I waited by the mailbox. Three weeks, four weeks. God, it was so excruciating, the anticipation, and I couldn't actually say for sure what it was I was waiting for, except that I'd heard these snippets of songs in a television ad—"Bo Diddley," "Ya Ya" by Lee Dorsey, "Whole Lotta Shakin' Goin' On" by Jerry Lee Lewis, all the way up to the Kingsmen's immortal "Louie Louie" and my treasured "Twist and Shout."

To get so many songs for seven dollars seemed like a bonanza to me. It finally arrived in this big cardboard box. I remember the multicolored cover, and that each label was a different color. There was no information, no liner notes or anything, only song titles and artists' names, and so many of them, most of them, were completely unknown to me, records primarily from before I was born, or when I was a toddler. Who were the Mello-Kings? Harold Dorman? My only disappointment was that the version of "Rock Around the Clock" by Bill Haley and the Comets was a lousy live recording, not the record I knew from the oldies station WCBS-FM. Even then, I was discerning and wanted only the certified originals. But I devoured that music.

*   *   *

By the summer of '72, rock pioneers like Elvis, Rick Nelson, and Chuck Berry were back on the charts with top-ten singles. I was quickly figuring out how much groups like the Stones and the Beatles owed to the artists I heard on the *Rock Is Here to Stay* album. This was all a part of my musical education, and I took it far more seriously than anything I was learning about US history or algebra: my Founding Fathers were Bo Diddley and Chuck Berry. My mathematic equations involved Frankie Lymon + the Teenagers, Dion + the Belmonts. Later I got *Nuggets*, the double album of '60s garage and psychedelic rock curated by Lenny Kaye on Elektra, and Sire's two-LP *History of British Rock*, spanning everything from Manfred Mann to Dusty Springfield to Donovan.

I was a sponge, and I gave everything a chance: southern rock like the Allmans, prog rock like King Crimson. I found T. Rex musically fascinating—the wordplay was sort of nonsensical but was perfect for the sense of rhythm; the language was percussive and seductive; and Tony Visconti's production was brilliant, the way he'd place Marc Bolan's voice and guitars in the mix. One night, decades later, I was sitting on a patio with Visconti and David Bowie in Little Italy, and Tony told me how he used to return to the studio after hours and layer on all the strings over the guitars. It was a unique sound, the element that made the records shimmer so memorably.

On the precipice of puberty I was drawn to glam rock: the sheer crass noize of Slade, Mott the Hoople's version of Bowie's "All the Young Dudes," even the stomping, retro feel of the singles Chinn and Chapman made with the Sweet.

You have no power over what rock generation you're born into, but there was something adventurous going on in the years of my musical (and hormonal) awakening. In the absence of one all-consuming musical trend, you could see some people looking over their shoulder, taking risks and bending the rules.

And it was a period of anatomical self-discovery. Music became the cultural outlet for all my desires, frustration, and daydreams regarding sex. And how fortunate that, as Hank Ballard and the Midnighters had done in the '50s, and the Rolling Stones had done in the '60s, we had bands whose music sonically emulated a hard-on, while at the same time we had reflective young singer-songwriters who tapped into our romantic confusion and longing. That's when you fall in love, and you're lust-dizzy, and you're always looking for the songs that articulate all that hormonal mess. It's all I thought about for almost every day of 1974. And there to provide the backdrop, the debut album by KISS; *Thunderbox* (there was a provocative title) by Humble Pie; *Get Your Wings* by Aerosmith; Thin Lizzy's *Nightlife*. Montrose. Bachman-Turner Overdrive. The New York Dolls' debut album.

In seventh grade I met a kid named Chuck Icenogle. The first British kid I'd ever met. He was from Liverpool, a total scouse, which of course made him even hipper. He was already close to six feet tall, with bright orange hair. He overheard me talking in the hall with someone else about music, so he approached me and invited me over to his house after school. Chuck's collection was a motherlode: he had KISS's debut, and Bowie's live album (I borrowed it from him), and glam singles by Gary Glitter and Slade (whose song "Cum On Feel the Noize" went on, in the hands of Quiet Riot, to launch a thousand hair-metal bands). His mom would go back to England once in a while to see her family, and every time she did, I'd give her twenty dollars and she'd buy whatever the top-ten singles in the UK were and bring them back to me—it didn't matter to me what they were, Brotherhood of Man, Rod Stewart, Elton John, I was fascinated by getting records that weren't available in the US. The labels were different, and the picture sleeves, and you didn't need a 45 adapter to play them: the holes in the records were smaller than on the American versions. That was my initial exposure to the British import single, and it began a habit that over the years had a very draining affect on my bank account. It all started with those twenty-dollar bills I gave to Chuck's mom.

My brother and I took the bus into New York City to see my first arena show at Madison Square Garden, Jethro Tull's stop on their War Child tour in March 1975. It wasn't my first live music experience: my mom and dad took me to Princeton to see Don McLean, whose "American Pie" record I liked because it was a song about rock 'n' roll, but his concert totally bored me, except for one song, "Narcissisma" (man, was he a pretentious cat or what?), where he showed *some* energy. Otherwise he was a yawn, so that wasn't exactly the best way to kick off my concertgoing life. I had higher expectations for Jethro Tull, because I knew "Aqualung" from the radio, and my sister-in-law had the *Benefit* album, which I loved. I know Jethro Tull has become a rock punch line because they won the first Grammy for Best Hard Rock/Metal Vocal or Instrumental in 1989, beating Metallica, Jane's Addiction, and AC/DC, but you can't blame that on them: they didn't submit themselves in the category, or vote for themselves. Grammy voters can be dense about rock. People tend to forget how important Jethro Tull were.

I psyched myself up for the show, listening to the *War Child* album, and I brought a little cassette recorder with me so I could document my first rock show.

We were all the way up in the rafters, and all around us kids were smoking weed. I was too distracted to pay much attention to the opening band, Carmen, but then Tull came out to the fanfare of classical music, and I'd never heard anything so loud: the powerful sound system, the cheering crowd. I was in the middle of—well, high above, really, but I felt part of it—this ear-splitting storm, and by the time they were into "Wind-Up" from *Aqualung,* I knew what an impact live rock music could have. Ian Anderson, doing flips onstage in his tights, doing these crazy acrobatics the whole time he was playing the flute: he knew how to roll over on his shoulder on the stage and not miss a note. Everything else is a blur—the audience, the hot dog guy yelling, they were off in the distance as far as I was concerned. I was intensely focused on that band onstage, so far away (this was before the big HD screens at arena shows now). Sometimes I think about that show, the first time I walked into the Garden and climbed all the way to the section farthest from the stage, and the two dozen times since then that I've stood on that same stage and introduced a band. I look up to the 300 level and imagine my thirteen-year-old self. At every show, there's someone who's never been to a concert before, who's looking at the spectacle with the same awe I felt when Glenn took me to the city to see Jethro Tull.

That was my gateway show, and decades later I told Ian Anderson how staggered I was by his presence onstage, and how I'd never before or since seen anyone play the flute like that. He said that at the start, Jethro Tull was another British blues band. "When I saw Eric Clapton play," he told me, "I realized I could never be as good as him, and wondered what I could do to be different. So I walked into a music store, looked around for a while, saw a flute, and said, 'Give me one of those.'"

At fourteen and fifteen, 1975 and into early 1976, I wanted to see as many rock shows as I could. Prior to that, my fixation was all about the records and the radio, but now I knew about this other dimension, the concert experience. Two shows stand out, for different reasons: Queen's Beacon show in February 1976 on the Night at the Opera tour, and Aerosmith's concert at Madison Square Garden that May on their Rocks tour. Let's get Aerosmith out of the way: they sucked. Aerosmith are one of the greatest American bands ever. I'd bought *Get Your Wings* in '74 because it had a cover of "Train Kept A Rollin'" on it, and in those days if a band did a song I liked (I knew that one from the Yardbirds' version), I'd take a chance on it. I loved that album, and the next one, *Toys in the Attic*, but things started to unravel on *Rocks*. But I stick with bands, and Aerosmith broke my heart that night. They were ragged, and the PA was crap. (Their next show, on the Draw the Line tour, I missed entirely when my friend and I were ejected from the Garden for erasing the seat numbers on our tickets to try and get a better view.) In later years, of course, Aerosmith had no peer as a US arena band, and I took my kid backstage to meet them. I told Joe Perry, "You crushed me when you did that tour for *Rocks*." He said, "We were so fucked up at the time. We were drinking and drugging, and we thought, 'We're still a garage band from Boston. We don't even need a good PA.'"

As disappointing as Aerosmith were at that point, Queen were transformative. That was a beautiful, life-changing show to see at fourteen, watching a band so unabashedly flamboyant, that embraced theatricality, that balanced hard rock and big melodies. They were the next step, with elements of glam and metal, and Freddie Mercury seemed brave to me, not in a sexual way—I didn't zero in on that any more than I did with the ambiguous implications of the New York Dolls in makeup on the cover of their debut album—but in the way that was unafraid of excess. *Night at the Opera* is the album with "Bohemian Rhapsody," and when that came out, it was dazzling and audacious. That's what the show felt like. I'd never seen a live band that sent me out into the street reeling like that, my teenage mind trying to wrap itself around what I'd just witnessed.

I'd yet to get my first blow job, but I had sex, and music, on my brain 24/7. I was already sneaking drinks in a cabin across the house from where I grew up in East Brunswick. The cabin was also where I and a few other friends who couldn't play any instruments worth a shit played our only gig as a band called the Diamond Back Four. I mean, we really couldn't play. My friends, who were three brothers, sort of banged away on guitar, bass, and drums, and I sang. We thrashed around. This was pre-punk, so we didn't have that as a fallback excuse for our ineptitude. The brothers lived in the cabin that their great-grandfather had built, like in the early 1900s, with a fireplace and a bar. It was the ultimate playhouse. We played our eight-track tapes and mixed Old Grand-Dad bourbon with lemonade in a Tupperware container. We took it outside to drink in a tent we'd set up in the yard, and I threw up for the next day and a half. I couldn't get out of bed. To this day, with all the liquor I've consumed over four decades, you could never get me near a shot of Old Grand-Dad; it would make me instantly nauseated. Maybe I should have sampled every brand of alcohol when

I was fourteen as aversion therapy. It would have saved me a bunch of stays in rehab.

You could party in the woods then, ride your bike around at night, try and catch frogs and Mayberry shit like that, except you could do it with alcohol and rock music. We'd bring our sleeping bags to an abandoned farm with these old chicken coops, paint the walls with the names of every favorite band, start a fire in a pit, and drink. Sometimes, we'd go to the Route 1 flea market and steal albums. We'd buy a few, so we had record bags, and then we'd lift three or four more. That went on for a few years, the record theft, until I got popped at Bradlee's department store and my brother had to come and get me. He didn't tell our parents, and I never shoplifted again; I had to find other ways to get my hands on all the music that was so essential to my psychic survival.

Encounters:
Lou Reed

Different records moved me in different ways, but from the time I saw his image sliced in half on the back cover of that third Velvet Underground album, I was fascinated by Lou Reed. I think I knew intuitively that he was a troublemaker, like me. That he pissed people off, and was confrontational. I was influenced by the fact that my brother liked him, and my brother was also someone who could raise hell.

When he was in high school, Glenn climbed the flagpole and pulled the American flag down to half-mast after Bobby Kennedy was killed. Glenn was smack in the center of the whole '60s scene, and I looked up to him so much. I hated to see him and my dad battle it out over the war, but my brother always was in my corner and feeding my music fix. If he liked an album, I was sure it was going to be cool. So when he brought home Reed's *Transformer,* the album that was produced by Bowie and had "Walk on the Wild Side," I knew I had to pay attention. Honestly, I can't explain why an eleven-year-old kid in New Jersey, even one as precociously moody and musically curious as I was, would find common ground with someone who sounded like the denizen of dark urban alleys. But I was hooked by the way Reed snapped out his lyrics, the insolent I-could-give-a-fuck-ness of his singing, the grit and sexuality. I might not have known what "giving head" was, I may have been taken aback by an album whose opening words were "Vicious, you hit me with a flower," I'd probably never heard the word *transsexual* in my short life, let alone met one, but on some primal level this preadolescent sixth grader realized that Lou Reed was expanding what pop and rock music could tackle. He was testing what listeners could handle. That's what excited me, I'm sure: the transgression. It's the same early thread that ran through garage rock and later punk, the idea that within the confines of a three-minute song you could chuck decorum and politeness out the window, make noise, and say things you weren't supposed to say out loud. It was as though *Transformer* was an album you had to listen to secretly, even though "Walk on the Wild Side" was all over the radio in the beginning of 1973. That seemed like a mistake, like someone at the station was asleep at the switch and played the song by accident.

From that point on, I followed every move Lou Reed made, even the least explicable ones. I went back to find the other Velvet Underground albums (*Loaded*, with "Rock and Roll" and "Sweet Jane," is one of the cornerstones of any collection of rock LPs). I bought *Berlin*, and *Rock N Roll Animal*, a great live album recorded at New York City's Academy of Music (later renamed the Palladium), where I'd spend so many nights as I got older.

Reed was a constant presence in my own rock 'n' roll life. In later years I'd go see him live all the time and, depending on the night, he could be either incredibly compelling or on the edge of destruction, or both. I found bootleg VHS tapes of him onstage, wrapping up his arm and shooting—or pretending to shoot—heroin. By that time, I was in a drug period of my own, speed and coke, but when I saw that I thought, Wow, this is fucked up. What he was up to was in some ways repellent, or subversive, but you couldn't not watch him. He was in his own zone.

I certainly had no idea what to expect when I met Lou Reed a lifetime later when I was at MTV. I'd heard such horror stories, especially from friends and rock journalists, who told me how witheringly brutal he could be, what an intimidating cat he was, how he had zero patience for trivial bullshit or lack of preparation. I went into the greenroom for my show *120 Minutes,* and right off the bat I explained to him that I've never been afraid to start a conversation with anybody, especially when their music is important to me. That was my icebreaker. I was feeling confident, and that's not arrogance or ignorance. I knew Lou's rep for ripping into people, and I forged ahead anyway, and he was different with me than in any article I've ever read, except maybe the *Creem* magazine pieces Lester Bangs did with him where they had these wildly entertaining sparring matches.

Maybe he'd seen me on TV before this, maybe he hadn't, but I had the feeling that he thought, Okay, this guy is not some jerk-off. I told him about hearing "Beginning to See the Light" when I was a kid and following his career, and we hit it off. He wanted to talk about everything: how Warhol would encourage him at the start of the Velvets and pushed him to keep writing more songs. How he was asked to be in the movie *I Shot Andy Warhol* and turned it down. "How can I be a part of a movie about my friend getting shot? I'd never do shit like that." He was my guest for the whole show, and I asked him about Bowie, and I have to say, he was very open and responsive, both in the greenroom before the taping and then during the interview that aired on *120.* By then he'd been through so much in his career, and he had a new record out, and it's safe to assume that he didn't know where he fit in at MTV. Even artists like Lou Reed need validation from time to time.

It's strange, but we stayed in touch after that. You wouldn't think Lou Reed would be that kind of person, but we would e-mail each other; he'd invite me to things. Maybe it was because he was older and mellower by then, but I continued to hear stories about how he'd eviscerate some underprepared interviewer, so I'm guessing he was prickly and unpredictable for the rest of his life. I had a TV show on HD-Net called *Sound Off* around '04, '05, and if you watch it, you can see the warmth between us. He's joking about some early gig he played at a Jersey high school, having fun, completely relaxed and un-Loulike.

Another time he came on my radio show to promote a live performance of *Metal Machine Music*. Talk about balls: when the album came out in 1975 it was roundly reviled as an exercise in self-indulgence, four LP sides of earsplitting feedback. No major rock star had ever released anything so brazenly uncommercial, with the possible exception of some of John and Yoko's more experimental things. I was a fourteen-year-old Lou Reed fan when it came out; I thought it was a great album title and he looked cool on the cover, and my neighbor had bought it on eight-track, which was then handed down to me. I gave it a listen and decided it was something he did to get his record label ticked off. Throughout his career, it was the one album most soundly panned, but he did not give one fuck. Thirty-five years later he was still defending it, and playing it live with a group called Metal Machine Trio. He had absolute belief in it, and on the air he compared it to classical music, calling it an important piece of work. Even though he was promoting a *Metal Machine* show, I still couldn't play any of that album on the radio. Listeners would have been injured lurching to change the station. I played "Sweet Jane" and "Vicious" and other classic Reed songs and gave him the platform to plug the *Metal Machine* experience. The one question I didn't ask him: "Did you really expect even your biggest fans to play *Metal Machine Music* all the way through?"

I didn't hear that Lou was ill, so when he passed away in October 2013, I was shocked. My girlfriend said she'd read online that he'd died. That's how death news is transmitted these days, and then the text messages and e-mails start flooding your inbox. It's instantaneous. The first person I heard from after my girlfriend was my friend actor-director Justin Theroux; sometimes he and I would walk around Washington Square Park with his dog, whom he'd named Lou Reed. He was the biggest Lou and Velvets fan I knew. I got a text: "Matt, I'm really mourning Lou today, but I'm mourning him in a good way because I love his music. And I can't think of Lou without thinking of you as well."

. . . And Then My Brain Exploded

Somehow I graduated high school

There I was in junior high, about to beat up my friend Michael (not his real name) over a girl. Let's call her Sue. Between the ages of thirteen and fifteen, I was obsessed with her. It finally came to a head when Michael and I got in a fistfight in the school bathroom, rolling around and beating the crap out of each other. We both got suspended. The only difference was, Michael's dad had "connections." When I went over to his house, there were pictures of his dad with Frank Sinatra and Sam Giancana.

"Wow, that's so cool your dad's with Frank Sinatra," I said, admiring the photo, not having any idea who the other gentleman in the picture was. Later on, I learned that he was a famed and feared member of the Mob, entwined not only with Sinatra but with JFK.

Michael's dad was probably proud of his son for getting into a fight. My dad was a physics teacher and the offensive line football coach of a high school in the same school system, so it was an embarrassment for him to have to come to school and get me. He drove over, took me back to the house, and told me, "Mow the lawn, and I'll see you when I get back from work!" Sure thing.

I dropped the lawnmower the minute he was out of sight and hitchhiked to Korvettes, a discount department store (it closed in 1980) that had a decent record department. They all did: Woolworth's, Grant's, Alexander's, Two Guys. Sometimes during sales you could get LPs for like $2.49. Since I had the rest of the day off, I went to where I could get records. What else was I going to do?

My sister-in-law Debbie was the manager of the record department. "I got a little birthday money," I told her. "What should I get?" This turned out to be a pivotal moment in my life, so mark it down: May 28, 1976.

"Well, I heard this band's really cool. They're called the Ramones."

She handed me the album. Four guys in leather. Classic black-and-white. Second from the right was this lanky dude with bad posture, wearing shades and torn-up jeans. I thought, Who the fuck is this? I turned it over, and the next thing that fascinated me (although really I was hooked by the photo; I'd have bought it anyway) was that there were fourteen songs. In those days most albums had ten, and it was also when bands like Yes would put out bloated albums like *Tales from Topographic Oceans*, with four songs on four sides. So for me, this was a rock economics lesson: for the same money, I get fourteen songs. Sold!

I brought home the first Ramones album, put it on the record player, and heard "Blitzkrieg Bop," and I thought, again, What the fuck? It sounded like the cover. I immediately loved it because it reminded me of the garage rock that I'd heard when I was a very young kid. Without the Ramones, no Sex Pistols, no Clash. It was life-changing. And it marked the first time that my friends and I started fracturing into musical camps. You had to take sides. Which I never understood, really. Loving one band, or one genre, shouldn't be such a tribal thing. One doesn't negate the other. I always wanted to take *everything* in.

But my friends were digging in their heels. Like when the Beatles came around, and there were kids who were so devoted to music by the Four Seasons and the Beach Boys that they took the British Invasion as a cultural affront. My friends who liked KISS or Alice Cooper got the Ramones, and could see what they were up to, stripping down rock to the bare minimum, not giving the audience a minute to breathe between songs, speeding everything up. No long solos, nothing complicated. It was a thrill ride, but not everyone wanted to get on. I heard, "What is this shit?" so many times.

And then my brain exploded. For real.

One morning, not long after my discovering the Ramones, someone in my homeroom, a girl named Debbie, came up to me and said, "Hey, Matt, what's that fucking thing on the side of your head?" I reached over.

"There's a bump."

"What?" I asked. I touched the side of my head and it was pulsating. I went home, and my mother took me to a neurologist who said, "Your son's not going to live." She didn't tell me this. She did tell the doctor she'd get a second opinion. I was fifteen.

She took me to the number-one neurosurgeon in the New Brunswick/Middlesex County area. We had to wait three hours to see him. The entire time I kept thinking, I could be home jerking off, or listening to rock 'n' roll, or chasing girls, or riding my bike.

When I found out I had to have surgery immediately, it didn't even register that this could be life-threatening. To me, it was more life-interrupting. No one told me how dangerous this was, and I didn't realize that all the visits to doctors were my parents' frantic attempt to find someone to give them a shred of hope. That's all they had to hold on to, and they barely got that.

I'd sit in those offices for hours at a time, waiting, primarily being annoyed rather than scared out of my wits, which I surely might have been if I'd been aware of what every prognosis was. Finally, there was a visit to a surgeon who thought the odds of a successful procedure were around 20 percent. That's something I didn't know then, that there was a four-in-five shot that I'd be dead before I turned sixteen.

It's mostly a blur to me, the whole period, but I do recall being in waiting room after waiting room, angry that I couldn't be outside, or playing my records. I had no idea that my mother was so terrified the night before the operation that she didn't even leave bedclothes for me at the end of my bed the way she usually did. God knows how she held it together for me. That night, I listened to the Kinks' *Schoolboys in Disgrace* album. That I do remember, and something by David Bowie, *Ziggy Stardust* or *Hunky Dory*.

"Hey, Matt," the neurosurgeon said the next day in the

hospital, "you know we're going to have to shave your head, so do you want us to shave half your head, or the whole thing?" What? The whole thing, I guess. Like, "Which alien do you want to be this week?" And all I was thinking about was how I was going to look when I got out, all those teenage girls I lusted after who'd be looking at me. That's what bothered me: the thought of being a bald teenager (although being a bald adult has worked out pretty well), and the thought of being out of circulation and missing out. It was more inconvenient for me than anything.

WNEW-FM, the New York City rock station, was playing when they were prepping me for this surgery. I was going under, my head was being cut into, and there was a solid chance the aneurysm was going to explode like a flash pot at a KISS concert. "Karn Evil 9 Second Impression" by Emerson, Lake and Palmer was playing as I lost consciousness.

"Welcome back, my friends, to the show that never ends," it goes. "Guaranteed to blow your head apart, we gotta see the show." That was the last thing I heard. "Guaranteed to blow your head apart."

The doctors stuck a tube down my throat, so I woke up with the sorest throat in the world. But I was alive. And thinking about this girl that I liked, Shelley (I wasn't in love with Sue anymore, you know how teenage shit goes), and about what it was going to be like to be a bald, scarred high school teenager. I didn't consider this a brush with mortality: I was angry at being taken out of the action. In ninth grade, I'd started singing in a band, Thunderhead, getting out my adolescent aggression by doing songs like "All Right Now," "Walk This Way," and "Can't Get Enough" (the standard riff-rock repertoire circa 1974–75), I had girlfriends, and I was pissed off that as the school year was coming to an end, my last year in junior high, I was in a hospital bed.

I was hospitalized for only a few weeks that July, but I was isolated from my friends, estranged from my record collection. I was lonely and cut off. My parents brought me copies of *Rolling Stone* and *Creem* magazine, *Circus* and *Hit Parader*. I was seeing early pictures of what was happening down at CBGB's on the Bowery in New York City, shots of the Ramones, Blondie, Talking Heads, Patti Smith. Talk about disorienting: I couldn't hear most of the music—some of those bands hadn't even released anything yet—but I could imagine it, or thought I could. Everything about it felt decadent and forbidding, so of course I wanted to be a part of it.

I emerged into the summer of '76 with a shaved head and stitches from one side of my skull to the other. I'd always felt alienated in a lot of ways, but now I looked the part, and I was hanging around with some pretty crazy kids. One of them was a horrible guy, a real dickhead, and he decided he wanted to wrestle. I wasn't into it, and I wasn't really up for it, but he insisted, and he ripped the bandage off my head. He was just fucking around, but I had to go back to the hospital for a couple of days to make sure the stitches were okay and everything was sanitary and uninfected. All of this right before I'm going to start high school, meeting all new people, being at the bottom of the school rung again. I went to a western store and bought a cowboy hat to cover my gash. A fucking cowboy hat, like Matt Dillon from *Gunsmoke*, or Wyatt Earp. It was the most ridiculous thing ever. Don't get me wrong: cowboy hats looked good on actual cowboys, and on country singers, and later on Bono, but this was '70s suburbia and no one, I mean no one, could walk through the streets of East Brunswick like it was Dodge City.

The transition back to reality was a tough one. Starting tenth grade means going to a new school, trying to blend in with kids from different junior high schools, so that September I walked through the halls and sat in the cafeteria feeling as though everyone's eyes were on me and I was a monster in their midst. I couldn't adjust, so my parents decided midterm to get me out of the public high school and send me to Rutgers Prep, a private school in Piscataway, around twenty miles from where we lived. That was a dark period for me; I met some kids in my new school, children of Jersey politicians, some of whom liked rock music and liked smoking weed, but I felt so out of place. Sometimes I wouldn't even go; I'd walk out of my house in the morning and just wander around. It was a weird time. Now not only did I look different, I wasn't even going to school with the kids from my neighborhood.

One morning I missed the bus. Snow was coming down and I was stranded, miles from the school, miles from home, in the middle of nowhere, and near the bus stop was an old junkyard. Not even a junkyard, really, with fences and guard dogs, but a crappy plot where people would abandon their cars because they simply couldn't be bothered. There was no way I could walk in either direction in the snow, so I climbed into one of those old rusted cars, with no windows and no tires, and sat there for what must've been at least four hours, quiet, cold, and alone, but raging inside at my cursed existence: What the *fuck* is going on?!? How did I wind up in a shell of a car in a snowstorm, trying to get to a school far from where I lived? What crime did I commit in a past life? The snow kept falling, maybe three feet, and finally it let up and I trudged the miles back home.

I look back on that post-op period as one of so much

anger and depression, and I don't know how I'd have gotten through it without the music that both reflected how I felt and opened a window into a new world. When you're young, you think your world, whatever crisis you're going through, that's the biggest thing ever, and the thing that saddens me is when I see kids throwing their lives away, doing stupid things and giving up on themselves. They've never had the chance to experience so many things, and they magnify their loneliness or insecurity and sink into a black hole. I get it. Those hours freezing in that shell of a car were like the end of the world, summing up all the injustice that had been imposed on me since I went into the hospital, but things turned around. I finished out that semester at Rutgers Prep, then went back to my local high school for my junior and senior years and got back into the groove. My hair started to grow back, I completely applied myself, got involved in the music department, even appeared in a senior play, *You Can't Take It with You.*

You know how in every high school class there's one car crash? That happened in my senior year, and because of that, I wasn't allowed to sing Elvis Costello's "Accidents Will Happen" in the school's variety show. My friend Jack and I were all prepared to do the piano version from the *Live at Hollywood High* EP, but we were told that it would be insensitive, so instead we did "Friend of the Devil" by the Grateful Dead and "Amie" by Pure Prairie League. I hated not being allowed to do the Elvis song, because I was such a big fan.

I found out that despite my abbreviated and rocky tenure at Rutgers Prep, I appear in the school's admissions video. After screening it recently to an incoming class, the headmaster felt obliged to add, "Well, Matt is not one of our typical students." No shit.

As always, records got me through. Bowie, Roxy Music, Springsteen. The Kinks. I felt like a monster, and those songs gave me a sense of my humanity. Naturally, a lot of the music I loved reflected what I was feeling, and my transformation happened to coincide with radical musical change. I was trying to absorb everything that was different, trying to connect with the New York punk world I was reading about in the music magazines. I'd already gotten hooked by the Ramones, and I also discovered the first album by Tom Petty and the Heartbreakers. They weren't really a part of that scene, but I was drawn to the attitude in songs like "Breakdown" and "Anything That's Rock and Roll." At a flea market I found a compilation LP from Holland called *Geef Voor New Wave*. Almost every song drilled into me: Eddie and the Hot Rods' "Do Anything You Wanna Do," Generation X's "Your Generation" (the first time I heard Billy Idol), the Adverts' "Gary Gilmore's Eyes." I could see the world changing, feel my life changing.

Some people reacted to the Ramones as though the band personally punched them in the face. That's what I was looking for. I wanted to be outraged and provoked. I wanted music to mirror how I felt, to see my soul's reflection in that shiny black vinyl of a new LP taken out of its shrink-wrap and placed carefully on the turntable. It's pretty common knowledge that the music we hear when we're around thirteen to fifteen years old is going to be the music we cling to through our adulthood. I was lucky to hit that age in time for the next big change.

I imagine it was like a fourteen-year-old turning on the radio in 1955 and hearing the music that disc jockey Alan Freed was playing—the erupting, grinding sound of early rock 'n' roll. But I was ready for music of my own. The world of mainstream pop, the songs you heard in supermarkets or if you were stuck in a car that only had an old AM radio, was all either slush (Chicago's "If You Leave Me Now," Manilow's unbearable "I Write the Songs," McCartney's "Silly Love Songs") or disco. I'm not one of those elitists who dismisses all disco music as a cultural travesty; a lot of the singles were vibrant and exciting. But, come on, it was week after week of "Disco Lady," "Boogie Fever," "(Shake, Shake, Shake) Shake Your Booty," "Play That Funky Music," "A Fifth of Beethoven," and the absolute low point, "Disco Duck." And a lot of rock music wasn't much better than "Get Up and Boogie." The year began with *Frampton Comes Alive!*, after all, and it was the era of Journey and the Doobie Brothers. The Stones' *Black and Blue* was hardly a highlight of their catalog.

In the middle of all this was music a misfit fifteen year old could find himself in: "Beat on the Brat," "Now I Wanna Sniff Some Glue," "Judy Is a Punk," "Loudmouth," played at four times the speed of normal rock 'n' roll, real grab-you-by-the-throat music. It wasn't 1976's only sign of life in a land dominated by corporate rock: Lou Reed and David Bowie released *Coney Island Baby* and *Station to Station*, and I was a fan of KISS's *Destroyer*, Aerosmith's *Rocks*, and Thin Lizzy's *Jailbreak*. Later in the year came *Howlin' Wind* by Graham Parker and the Rumour and the debut by Tom Petty and the Heartbreakers. And on July 4, 1976, the day of America's bicentennial, the Ramones played their debut concert in the UK, opening for the Flamin' Groovies at the Roadhouse, and you can date that as the night that punk began exploding in England. That same night, the Clash played their first-ever gig, opening in Sheffield for the Sex Pistols, and the night after, the fifth, the Ramones did a show at Dingwall's that brought out almost every punk band in the vicinity: members of the Pistols, the Clash, the Damned, the Stranglers, the Adverts. It was one of those moments when a scene becomes a movement. By that point, I had been living with the Ramones' debut album for about six weeks, completely in its thrall, and I was prepared for everything that came in its loud, ground-shaking wake.

There wasn't a punk or new wave single I didn't want to know about. I was completely hooked. As a young person who has all this pent-up energy, all this sexual drive, coming after my aneurysm, I wanted something that cut right to me. I wanted my heart to race.

We were at the breakfast table one morning and my mom said, "I just heard about this terrible band who are spitting on journalists. They were coming off the plane and spitting in their faces!" I looked at her and went, "I've got to hear that band!" It offended my mother so much that I had to find them. That's how it works. It's how it's always worked.

Like how in the Soviet Union, they were kicking kids out of college and imprisoning them for being found with anything Beatles-related. When I met Paul McCartney, I told him about a documentary, a propaganda film where the narrator is saying, "Look at these buffoons! They have toilet seats around their necks!" (They were actually life preservers, in a scene from *Help!*) And Paul said, "Of course, when they thought it was toilet seats around our necks, they wanted to hear us more." There you go.

That's what chasing down the Sex Pistols was for me. I was working at a party rental place, cleaning chairs, delivering tables, and nearby on the highway was a record store called Record Setter, which was getting imports. I bought

"God Save the Queen" and "Anarchy in the UK." They were the loudest fucking thing to come through my stereo in years. Those early chords were like a jackhammer. They moved me. I was immediately in love with the Sex Pistols. So when "Pretty Vacant" came out, I bought it too, and I was holding it in my hand when two older kids came pulling up to me in their car.

"Dude! You like punk rock!?"

"Yeah, I love it, man. I love the Sex Pistols, the Ramones . . ."

"Have you heard the Dead Boys?"

I hadn't. "Dude, you got to check out the Dead Boys!" I went back inside and the clerk played me "Sonic Reducer." So I bought *Young Loud and Snotty*, and that was it. I was locked into that music within seconds, and it became a big part of my life.

I was so into punk and new wave and just being a pain in the ass. I brought Dead Boys, Sex Pistols, and Ramones records to my music appreciation class, and people were screaming, just howling in disgust, running out of the classroom with their fingers in their ears. I was being confrontational, and it was definitely on purpose; I knew exactly what I was up to. Not all music brings people together: the Beatles did, for sure, and I discovered that I could unite the hippies and the new wave crowds by playing Tom Petty and the Heartbreakers. But I also knew, and liked, that music could be so polarizing. I saw the humor in that. I wanted to shake people up who might only own the *Saturday Night Fever* and *Grease* soundtracks. I knew there were certain people in that class who wouldn't "appreciate" what I was going to play for them, but I also thought, Hey, I've got a platform here, and the chance to play five songs, why not shake things up?

Encounters:
The Ramones

I never jumped off the Ramones train. It's one of those things where you stick with a band because they mattered so much to you at a pivotal point in your life. I didn't get to see them live until 1978, on the Road to Ruin tour, the one where Marky Ramone replaced Tommy. By the time I caught up with them, they were at the height of their popularity with "I Wanna Be Sedated." It looked as though the world had caught up with them, and at least a segment of the audience had: they were playing bigger and more packed venues, and the crowds were boisterous. The band's breakneck sprint through their sets suddenly didn't seem quite so foreign in the post-punk/early new wave world. In '78, with Blondie and Talking Heads becoming more and more popular, Elvis Costello releasing *This Year's Model*, Patti Smith getting her commercial breakthrough with "Because the Night," when I stood in the club watching the Ramones live, finally, after living so intimately with their records, I was convinced that they were going to be huge. I was right, in terms of their place in history; they're probably one of the three or four most significant bands in rock who never had a platinum album.

I met Marky at CBGB's around '79–'80, not long after he'd replaced Tommy. The first thing out of his mouth: "Name me three Ricky Nelson songs." It was like the question you have to answer before the troll lets you over the drawbridge.

"Uh, 'Travelin' Man.'" That was one. Shit. "'Be-Bop Baby.'" Come on, one more. "'Hello Mary Lou.'" Whew. I passed.

"All right, man. Buy me a drink."

That's how Marky and I became friends. He started calling me Matty Ramone, which is quite an honor.

The first time I met the rest of the band, we were shooting a concert for MTV. Before the show I went backstage to say hi. You know how, in *Rock 'n' Roll High School,* the Ramones are eating pizza, and P.J. Soles has a fantasy where she's feeding Joey pizza? That was their thing. So what were they doing backstage when I see them? Eating pizza, shoving it in their mouths, and I thought, How perfect, just like in the movie. I introduced myself and told them what a fan I was. But it wasn't until later on, when I was more visible on MTV, that I got to know Joey well. He called me at MTV and said, "It's so cool seeing somebody who really knows music on television. I remember you and I talked about when you bought our first record. If you ever need anything, give me a call."

Joey was amazing, because from then on he was always there for me. When I started hosting a show I conceived called *Rocks Off,* where guests come on and rap about videos, I needed people to come on, and I said to Joey, "It's not a high-priority show, so we have to tape at seven *a.m.*" What rock star wants to be anywhere at seven *a.m.*? But he showed up, and I took him out to eat afterward. We got burgers and talked. About records, '60s songs like the ones the Ramones did on the *Acid*

Eaters album, "Time Has Come Today," "Psychotic Reaction." Records that influenced both of us so much.

We became friends. We always talked about stuff that was going on in our lives. I was going through a rough period when I was in California, and I was not in good shape. It was probably at the Bel Age on Sunset in LA. I'd been drinking and getting high, with musician friends who wanted to go nuts. I felt like shit, and I knew I had to do something about it, so I called Tim Armstrong from Rancid. At the time he was seeing Brody from the Distillers, and they lived in the Silver Lake neighborhood. Tim said, "Dude, I'm getting you out of your hotel. Come over to my place, I got a huge record collection you can go through." So he and Brody picked me up and we grabbed some Thai food. He pulled me out of what was a hairy situation.

When I got home, I got a call from Joey. "Hey, Matt, I talked to Tim, man. I'm worried about you." That's how he was. He gave a shit.

"I don't want you to kill yourself. I know everyone in the world wants to party with you because you're on TV and on the radio and you're the rock guy. But this shit is going to fucking kill you. We love you, we care about you, man."

We'd sit on the phone for an hour and a half, two hours, having intense conversations about the all-time best 45s of the '60s. Going through everything we loved, British Invasion records, garage records. That's how he talked me down. He was worried because Tim had told him how messed up I was, and

57

the whole community of punk dudes, they watch out for each other, like looking out for members of their club. Tim didn't say, "Joey, you should call Matt," like it was an intervention thing. It was Joey being a friend, and the crazy thing about that was we would talk all the time, but he never let on that he was getting sick. He was concerned about me, but I had no idea how ill he was.

It was Bono who told me Joey was sick, when I was in Ireland with U2. At their Irving Plaza show they dedicated "I Remember You" by the Ramones to Joey.

Joey would never let on to me what was up. He'd dodge questions or downplay. "Oh, man, you know, I'm not feeling the best, but I'm hanging in there." He was slowly working on a solo record. I had gone down to Jacksonville, Florida, to be with my ex-wife's family when I got the news that Joey had died. I'd kept thinking in that hopeful way that this was going to be fixable, that he would go into remission and be okay.

What I think about a lot—besides Joey's generosity and spirit and kindness—is how his and the other Ramones' vision for the band has been validated by history. All those kids who ran screaming from the room when I played Ramones records, all the meatheads who hated punk and called it unmusical garbage, they're all chanting, "Hey! Ho! Let's go!" at ball games, and hearing the Ramones in car commercials. Joey knew the Ramones were a great American rock band, but I think he felt their legacy was unsettled. Joey died in 2001, and a year later

Eddie Vedder from Pearl Jam inducted the Ramones into the Rock and Roll Hall of Fame. Of all people, Joey would have appreciated that moment, the sweet irony of being embraced by a music industry that initially tried to marginalize them. In his speech, he probably would have thanked bands like the Seeds and the Count Five, who will probably never get into the Hall of Fame but have contributed so much to real rock 'n' roll.

Every year I hosted tribute concerts for Joey on his birthday. Joey's mom, Charlotte, whom I loved, came up to me one night and hugged and kissed me and said, "Matt, thank you for all the energy you put into honoring the memory of Joey." It's the least I could do for someone who changed my life and always did his best to see that I saved it.

The Joy of Access:
Getting in the Door

S ome kids at my school loved new wave and punk rock as
much as I did. Finding your gang, that's so key. Like the
kids in the show *Freaks and Geeks*: you gravitate to people
who make you feel more secure in your passions, especially when you know there are other kids who are going to
mock you. That's a thing about high school. You're pigeon-
holed by what you wear, whether you're a stoner or a jock,
whether or not your parents have money. So you group
together, and that becomes your world. All you need is a
few like-minded friends, and I was lucky to have my running partners.

Records were no longer enough for me. I wanted to get
closer, be in the room. I didn't want to be a passive fan. I felt
incomplete somehow, like I wasn't getting the whole story,
like the objects I could hold in my hand and study and play
on my stereo suggested I could access something bigger
and more profound. I wanted to know all the secrets: Who
were the people who made this, what drove them, influenced them? What was the *process* of rock music? I needed
it explained to me: first, just so I could be more informed,
and second, to share what I found out.

* * *

What I had to do was start going to shows, be in the audience, and then, ultimately, to be backstage. I get the seductive power of the backstage pass, the sticker to slap on your jeans, the laminate to drape around your neck. It's the power of proximity. I knew some girls wanted to get those passes so they could get into the dressing room to suck rock-star dick; that was part of rock mythology, that it was a world of blow jobs. If you're sixteen or seventeen years old, a world of blow jobs is where you want to become a citizen. But I didn't want access to get head. I thought that maybe, before some girl got on her knees to service a British bass player, he might have a few seconds to tell me what inspired him to come up with the lick on a cut buried on side two of the band's third album. I couldn't offer anything in return, certainly not what the girls could. But if I could get his attention, I could impress him with how much I knew about what he very well may have already forgotten. (In later years, I often found that I remembered much more about when and how an album was made than the people who made it.)

As soon as I could, I started going to shows. Before there was Ticketmaster, decades before you could buy tickets online, before you even knew where to find a scalper, there would be ticket outlets scattered around the city, at record stores, at luncheonettes. And some simpleminded Cro-Mag fucking Neanderthal with no brains and no taste would be behind the counter, and you'd be waiting on line for tickets. You would stand there, and this guy would look at you like you were crazy if you bought tickets for some shit he'd never heard of. Like he was a musical security guard.

My friend Greg Amicci and I went to one of these stores and asked for tickets for a Police show.

"Police? What kind of fucking band name is that? Who the fuck are the Police?" Greg and I exchanged disbelieving glances.

"You know," he continued, "you better enjoy this concert because these motherfucking guys are going nowhere."

Okay. Thanks for the heads-up.

The show was at the Walnut Theater in Philadelphia, and tickets were two bucks. We were only three rows back, and the show was being simulcast on WIOQ in Philly. They had one album out at the time, so they had to stretch. Sting starts singing "Roxanne," the hook, for what feels like forever. I was getting a little irritated by hearing "ROX-anne! ROX-anne!," so while the audience was going "ROX-anne," I decided I was going to sing a different song, one I'd discovered only because the band was from Athens, Georgia, where I was born, and I had to buy it. How many singles said "Athens, GA" on them? Sting and the audience kept singing "ROX-anne," and I bellowed "Rock LOB-ster!" And it became this battle. Now everybody in my row was going "Rock LOB-ster!" and finally Sting sang, "Not Rock Lobster!" And this was being broadcast on the radio. I still have the cassette. "Roxanne" went on for about fifteen minutes, and they played "Can't Stand Losing You" twice.

People forget how punk the Police were. Not musically—although their debut single "Fallout" certainly qualifies as a punk record—but in their whole presentation. The single sleeve of "Can't Stand Losing You" was truly disturbing. On the front cover is a guy standing on a block of ice with a rope around his neck. On the back the ice has melted and his legs are dangling there, and there's a picture of the band lying in the water, next to a space heater. The song sounds like this happy pop-reggae thing, and there's this suicidal image on the 45.

Greg and I hung out with the Police after their set. We waited by their bus, and when they came out I said, "Man, we love your record. 'Truth Hits Everybody,' that's the best song on the album." (I couldn't say one of the singles, because I had to show I wasn't a casual fan: I took this *seriously*.) Very few people, at that point, gave a shit. A lot of punk and new wave bands were psyched when they had fans that actually wanted to meet them. Sting, Andy, and Stewart took some pictures with us, and I talked to them a while. It came easy to me. I wasn't nervous or intimidated. And it showed me that if you approach musicians on a level of respect and with genuine interest and knowledge, they'll let you into their world for a while. Rock stars—or in this case, almost rock stars—were approachable. Even beyond that, they were happy to spend time with people who had appreciated their music.

Here's what motivated me: I always wanted to tell every fucking artist whose records I loved why I loved them and why they were great. I always believed my opinion mattered. And it did, to the people around me, even in my small microcosm of a world. I needed to hear a story and share a story. That became my thing, that one-to-one connection of looking the artist in the eyes, getting him or her to open up to me.

* * *

That same weekend of the Police show, we saw Joe Jackson and Elvis Costello and the Attractions at the Princeton University gym. Jackson was hitting it kind of big with *Look Sharp!* and the song "Is She Really Going Out with Him." It was one of many times at the Fast Lane in Asbury Park that I tried to sneak backstage, and the bouncer would go, "What're you doing back here?" and the artist would go, "No, no, he's cool. Let him through." I would quickly say something to engage them so that I wouldn't get thrown out. I was only a teenager, but I was that aggressive. I never asked for an autograph or souvenir or any of that shit. I just wanted to talk about the records and walk away with something—not something tangible, but real. A moment where the artist and I clicked.

Elvis Costello was really nasty to the audience at the Princeton gym. He was a provocateur by nature, belligerent by virtue of the booze. That was a rough patch for him: in March 1979, he'd gotten into a notorious altercation with Stephen Stills and Bonnie Bramlett, a verbal brawl that included, on Elvis's part, an ugly racial remark about Ray Charles. It was reckless, and he immediately regretted it—he was just trying to bait his combatants, and it got out of hand—but the incident was still fresh in people's minds when he played at Princeton a month later, so when he opened his set with his cover of "I Stand Accused," most of the people in the college crowd knew what he was referencing. It was that kind of scalding set, filled with his most brittle songs ("Goon Squad," "Two Little Hitlers," "Green Shirt"), and he was in no mood for requests (I think someone yelled out for "Alison," which he didn't do) or encores. The screwed-up thing is, Elvis is steeped in American soul music, revered Ray Charles, and if it weren't for that unfortunate outburst, you can imagine them doing duets later on, maybe on a Costello song like "Almost Blue." Ray would've nailed that one down.

I was nobody, sure. I wasn't a willing blonde with great tits, or a drug dealer with supply to share, or a label executive who could make things happen. I had nothing to offer, and only had seconds to convince a band member that I was okay. Like when Ian Hunter was playing at the Fast Lane, and Mick Ronson was on guitar, I made a beeline for the dressing-room door when the bouncer wasn't looking. I started talking to Ronson about his records with Bowie, and how much I dug Mott the Hoople, Hunter's band, and Mick handed me his guitar, let me start tuning it, strumming it. Once the bouncer saw me, he flipped out, but Ronson, bless his soul, one of the major guitar players, goes, "Ah, no, he's good. He's with us."

"He's with us" is one of the best sentences ever. It means the fucking world to me. Aren't we all looking for that type of acceptance, that brotherly embrace, that confirmation of cool? Ronson handing me his guitar took on symbolic weight.

People wonder about me, coming out of suburban New Jersey, with no relatives in the music business—what was it that permitted me to make that jump? The thing is, no one gave me permission to do anything. I just had balls, and knew how to seize brief moments. I knew how to make an impression. I was a high school kid who thought nothing of going to the Empire Hotel in Manhattan, where I heard Gary Numan was staying (this was when "Cars" was a big hit), wait for him to come down, and start talking to him. The next moment he was asking me to come sit with him and his parents where they were having dinner.

Or I would sneak backstage at the Palladium at a Boomtown Rats concert and walk right up to Andy Warhol and say, "Andy, man, I love your cover for *Love You Live.*" That's how I approach Warhol. I have no fear. I'm talking to him about those cutout pictures of the Stones for that album cover, and he gets a kick out of me. He was just giggling. He found me humorous, this ballsy kid. I asked him if he was going to the Boomtown Rats party, and I asked him for a ride. The nerve of me, right? He said sure, and I wound up in Warhol's limo and getting into this party and talking with Rick Derringer from the McCoys and Johnny Winter's band, and David Johansen, who'd been in the New York Dolls. This is stuff a normal teenage kid is not going to do.

Even before the Brain Incident (note: good band name or album title), I was a moody kid who was filled with angst and layers of complex emotion, and in my case that meant that I looked for music that churned me up, music that sounded the way I felt. That could have easily turned me into a Metal Kid, hanging out with the stoners who loitered at the Dairy Queen parking lot blasting AC/DC's *Let There Be Rock.* Or I could have ripped open a six-pack, put on headphones, and let Led Zeppelin's *The Song Remains the Same* pound at my already fragile skull. I liked those bands and KISS, whose *Love Gun* also ruled in the summer '77, but as much as I was drawn to the riff-heavy macho ejaculation of '70s hard rock, I made a deeper connection to bands like the Jam, the Ramones, and the Clash. They spoke to me more directly; I felt that they were working-class guys like me, frustrated, bored, whose only means of expression was lobbing these musical grenades. The effect on me was instant. If you're reading this and you aren't familiar with the Jam, put the book down this fucking minute, download the 2015 Jam compilation *About the Young Idea*, and don't come back until you've listened to all forty-seven tracks, starting with the 1977 single "In the City." Sometimes you find the exact music you need at exactly the right time.

They were coming out to kill, those bands. I saw the Jam three times in one week, one of the greatest live bands ever. From that period, I'd say no one could touch them or the Clash.

Every messed-up seventeen-year-old boy needs an outlet for all that bottled-up undefined rage. I found mine in the Jam's *All Mod Cons* album that came out near the end of 1978, surely one of the greatest albums of that era—and it's strange, in a way, that it hit me so directly, because it was so steeped in things British. Even the song titles are culturally specific: "Down in the Tube Station at Midnight," " 'A' Bomb in Wardour Street," "English Rose." But it transcended that; it went beyond what was called the Mod Revival. Paul Weller's songs were incredible, and I could trace the line from the Kinks' "A Well Respected Man" to Jam songs like "Mr. Clean." That track wasn't a single and probably got very little airplay, if any, but I loved it. It was unfiltered; it had a primal power that any disaffected kid can relate to. It was music that snarled, and I always liked music that had that attitude, like you could almost see the singer sneering while he sang. That insolence is liberating, and it's what I heard on *All Mod Cons* and on some tracks on the second Clash album, *Give 'Em Enough Rope*, that came out at the same time.

And then there were all the post-punk bands that followed: Joy Division's *Unknown Pleasures* in '79, the first album by the Cure, also in '79, then Echo and the Bunnymen, the Teardrop Explodes. My late adolescence, the end of the '70s and start of the '80s, was streaked with black. I guess these bands—and even lesser-known bands like the Sound and the Comsat Angels, most of whom I discovered by buying import records—were like my generation's Velvet Underground. Gloomy outsider music. But I also got a kick out of some purely dumb and crazy records, like the stupid "Making Bacon"/"Tight Pussy" import 45 by UK punk band the Pork Dukes. It was idiotic, but at sixteen, you think it's so subversive. We used to play that single in high school and laugh our asses off. When the Dead Kennedys came along, I had to buy the record no matter what it was, just because of the sheer balls it took to name a band the Dead Kennedys. I mean, the '60s had the Fugs and David Peel; we had bands like the Pork Dukes, the records you'd sneak into school and show to your friends and laugh about. You can't defend records like that musically, but part of the rock experience growing up is the shock value. That's why all that hysteria from Tipper Gore and the Parents Music Resource Center and the movement to sticker albums was so ludicrous, with senators being shocked over lyrics like "sniff my anal vapors" and reciting them in Congress. I laughed hysterically, because no one would have even heard of that stupid record otherwise. After Congress made such an issue of it, a friend of mine bought it and played it for me. If it gets adults worked up, you know you have to hear it. The outrage brigade just makes kids want to hear it even more.

Encounters:
Billy Idol

I was such a huge fan of Generation X that I actually wore a handmade *Valley of the Dolls* T-shirt in honor of that album. You couldn't buy punk band merch back then, so I made one myself and wore it to my high school graduation rehearsal. They had terrific songs: "Ready Steady Go," "Your Generation," "Kiss Me Deadly." Only the kids who were cool knew about them.

Then Billy Idol went solo, and he had an EP out with "Mony Mony," "Baby Talk," and "Dancing with Myself." And he was about to put out the album with "White Wedding" and "Hot in the City." He was playing at this place called the Red Fox Inn on Route 27 in New Jersey. Artists who were sort of on the margins played there. It was like in North Brunswick, on a side road. A small club, maybe two hundred capacity, three hundred max. My friend, I'll call him L.B., and I were there to see Idol, and of course we wanted to get backstage. What I realized was that if you acted as though you belonged there, sometimes you could sail right through security (truthfully, there wasn't much in the way of a screening process at these out-of-the-way venues, usually just some bored guy too distracted by checking out girls to worry about a couple of kids). It was basically a hustle: "Hey, I'm here from the Rutgers station and we're supporting the show and I need a few minutes . . . " Blah-blah. It wasn't as though we were trying to sneak into the Stones' dressing room at Madison Square Garden, or the VIP section of Studio 54; this was a joint on Route 27. Sure, kid, go on in. Easy.

L.B. had got them this big bag of cocaine. He was a couple years older than me and was friends with a lot of music industry people. He knew that having blow would get him backstage. This was the first time I got high with him.

Meanwhile, I was jazzed to be talking with Billy, about Gen X and all that, and then L.B. said, "Come in here with us."

We went into this little bathroom in the dressing room. Obviously, you couldn't share with everyone. Coke was fucking expensive. I wanted to spend all my money on records and live shows and gasoline for my car to get me to those shows, and maybe some beers if no one else is buying. That was it. I didn't have any discretionary drug money, which was probably a good thing.

I remember my brother had collected, from when he was a little boy, these little plastic baseball bats, Louisville Sluggers with the teams' names on them. I saw something that resembled one of those things in the bathroom at the club and thought, What's he got that for? Then all of a sudden he pressed on it, and a little fucking spoon came out of the bottom of it, a scoop, and it scooped up some blow. It's got a hole in the top, so you stick this fucking mini–baseball bat up your nose and snort the coke. So he's giving me and Billy Idol this shit, we're feeling good, we're drinking, getting wasted, just me and Billy talking. The madness was, of course, just starting.

Billy was wild in those days. Because, look, he comes from London, and all those punk bands did cheap speed. They would break open these capsules and snort. That's all the punks could afford then. That's how they would play so fucking fast and be sweating and going bananas onstage. Billy was a handsome guy on the brink of world fame. Everyone was offering him drugs, and no one, not on the east side of New Jersey in any case, was around to chaperone him. I'm so glad there were no smartphones back then, because if a picture ever showed up of me with a little Louisville Slugger up my nose, I'd never live it down.

This was before MTV, and the video of "White Wedding" that made Billy a megastar. I was at Rutgers at this point, interviewing everyone that played the school and the nearby clubs. When I heard that Billy and A Flock of Seagulls were coming in for a show, we booked them to come to the station for interviews.

I waited. And waited. And asked the college label reps where the hell he was. It turned out he was fried from a night in New York City, and they asked me, "Can you come over and get him? He's at the student center doing sound check."

I got there and Billy was extremely hungover. His manager was with him, guiding him like a seeing-eye dog to the elevator, which would bring him to the campus radio station. The news director, a college kid and big Billy Idol fan, miked him in the control room. Then Billy turned to me and said, "Hey, man, is it cool if we do some coke? I have to wake up."

His tour manager poured it out on a desk, and Billy and I did lines before the interview. The news director, poor kid, it was like somebody gutted him with a knife. He couldn't believe what he was seeing.

"I'm ready," Billy said. "Let's go!" He was so burnt that the only way he could equalize himself was to do that. He'd probably been up all night, and sometimes it's really hard to say, "Nah, I'm good," when fans want to turn you on. It seems really exciting and fun, and it is, until it isn't.

50 ESSENTIAL ROCK ALBUMS:
THE '70s

AC/DC—*Highway to Hell*

Aerosmith—*Toys in the Attic*

The Allman Brothers Band—*At Fillmore East*

Big Star—*Radio City*

Black Sabbath—*Paranoid*

Blondie—*Parallel Lines*

The Boomtown Rats—*A Tonic for the Troops*

David Bowie—*The Rise and Fall of Ziggy Stardust and the Spiders from Mars*

The Buzzcocks—*Singles Going Steady*

Cheap Trick—*In Color*

The Clash—*London Calling*

Alice Cooper—*Love It to Death*

Elvis Costello and the Attractions—*This Year's Model*

Dead Boys—*Young Loud and Snotty*

Deep Purple—*Machine Head*

Bob Dylan—*Blood on the Tracks*

Marvin Gaye—*What's Going On*

Generation X

Grateful Dead—*American Beauty*

Joe Jackson—*Look Sharp!*

The Jam—*All Mod Cons*

KISS—*Hotter Than Hell*

John Lennon—*Plastic Ono Band*

Lynyrd Skynyrd—*(Pronounced 'Lĕh-'nérd 'Skin-'nérd)*

Paul McCartney and Wings—*Band on the Run*

Joni Mitchell—*Court and Spark*

Van Morrison—*Moondance*

Mott the Hoople—*Mott*

Gary Numan and Tubeway Army—*Replicas*

Tom Petty and the Heartbreakers—*You're Gonna Get It!*

The Police—*Outlandos d'Amour*

Queen—*Sheer Heart Attack*

Ramones

Lou Reed—*Transformer*

The Rolling Stones—*Exile on Main Street*

Roxy Music—*Greatest Hits*

Sex Pistols—*Never Mind the Bollocks, Here's the Sex Pistols*

Sly and the Family Stone—*There's a Riot Goin' On*

Patti Smith—*Horses*

Southside Johnny and the Asbury Jukes—*Hearts of Stone*

The Specials

Bruce Springsteen—*Darkness on the Edge of Town*

Steely Dan—*Can't Buy a Thrill*

T. Rex—*The Slider*

Talking Heads—*Fear of Music*

Thin Lizzy—*Jailbreak*

Johnny Thunders and the Heartbreakers—*L.A.M.F.*

Van Halen—*Van Halen II*

The Who—*Quadrophenia*

Stevie Wonder—*Innervisions*

XTC—*Drums and Wires*

Yes—*The Yes Album*

Music Appreciation 101:
Majoring in Rock Studies

Outside the Melody, getting ready to spin

I got my first club spinning job at a go-go joint called JK's Talk of the Town. It was like the Bada Bing on *The Sopranos*. I'd help pick the strippers' music, and they'd throw me some tip money if I played things they liked. I played a lot of "Her Strut" by Bob Seger. I was making around eight bucks an hour, but there were other benefits. If they liked the music I played, and they got more tips, a) they'd throw me extra money and b) we'd hook up. There was a motor lodge right next door called the Host Ways, so we'd go in there and get a room, or, if there were no rooms available, we'd improvise. The club closed around two a.m., and the girls and I were always still wired. I wasn't making much cash, but I got to play music all night, watch hot girls take their clothes off, get smashed, and have sex. I recommend it highly as a college job.

When I wasn't DJing or going to school, I was working part-time as a security guard. My girlfriend at the time waited tables, and after her shifts, she'd pick me up and we'd check into a cheap hotel in North Brunswick. We'd bring snacks that I stole from the convenience store, get stoned, fuck, put on the TV for a while, then go back to our families the next day for Sunday-night dinner. She was cool, a big fan of the Rolling Stones. One Friday night, we were in bed watching *Don Kirshner's Rock Concert.* Prince performed "Controversy" and "Sexuality." I was always looking for other black music to play at the strip club. So I thought, Hmmm, I might need this for the dancers. I was really converted into a Prince fan by the *Controversy* album; he was an amalgam of James Brown and Hendrix, on another plane of sexuality and spirituality. Then *1999* tore my head off. I flipped over it. I know it sort of got overshadowed by *Thriller,* which came out around the same time and took over the planet, and I loved parts of that album too, but for me, it was Prince that was really pushing everything forward.

Mostly the strip club was an easy gig, and I was having a good time, but what I really wanted to do was get into radio for real. I wanted to be a DJ on a station like WLIR on Long Island or KROQ in Los Angeles. I was hearing about these stations but had no idea how to get a radio job. It bummed me out. I didn't have an in. No uncle or cousin who could get me through the door. I thought it was nearly impossible, but I was going to keep trying to meet people until I got an opportunity. That was my end game.

Let me backtrack a little, to my first time on college radio. It would have been normal to wait until I was actually *in* college to make my debut, but I was way too impatient for a sequence of events that conventional. Because the Rutgers station was always holding pledge drives, they decided to offer a chunk of air time to listeners who donated. That was the perfect situation for me. So my high school friends and I scraped up the required amount of money to buy that time on the air—ten to midnight on a Tuesday. When my "shift" arrived, I was ready: I wasn't going to use the Rutgers album library; I brought in all my own records. I knew what order I wanted to play them, when I would break to back-announce (tell listeners what songs they'd just heard), and talk about the songs and the bands.

I was too excited to be nervous, because in my mind I'd been preparing for this opportunity since I was in grade school. It sounds insanely cocky, I know, that at sixteen I could walk into a radio station thinking, I got this. Who did I think I was? Just someone who belonged behind a mic, I guess. A shaper of minds, a friendly guide, the loudest and most informed voice in the room. A high school student with a cool collection of records that he wanted to play for the masses.

This was my real debut, apart from the AM transmitter in my basement. I played "Mystery Dance" from the first Elvis Costello album, "Thunder and Rain" by Graham Parker and the Rumour, "Truth Hits Everybody" by the Police. I knew some of my friends would want to hear the Grateful Dead— and I loved them too—so I spun "U.S. Blues." And something by the Boomtown Rats. My friends at home taped my set on an eight-track. Matt's First Show, 1977. I had an engineer in the studio with me, and during the show he said, on the air, "Man, I can't believe how good you are." He was shocked, but dude, I was ready. I had been ready.

Not long after that, I applied for an on-air job there. Except, uh, I wasn't a Rutgers student yet, and the thing about being on college radio, the whole point of it, really, is that it's a program for the people who in fact attend the school. I suppose I should have taken that into account, but I'd figured since I'd done so well in the slot I paid for, they might bend the rules a bit and make an exception. They didn't. But they were nice about it, and told me to come back when I was enrolled at Rutgers.

Okay. That seemed fair. But my parents weren't ready to send me to Rutgers straight away. To be honest, they weren't sure I was going to put in the necessary work to take advantage of a college education, and I can't blame them for being skeptical, considering my high school track record of prioritizing rock music listening over homework doing. And they were only marginally aware, I think, of the other things that took precedence in my teenage life: weed smoking, sex pursuing, beer drinking—since my brain surgery, I'd become the designated buyer of brew. All this didn't bode well for a regimen of higher education. So as a trial, I went for a year to Middlesex Community College.

Middlesex sort of had a radio station. No, "radio station" is way too generous a term. There was a room in the school where you could play records that reached an audience consisting of whatever students happened to be eating lunch in the cafeteria at that moment. That was our demographic: hungry community college students who wanted to eat indoors. On a sunny afternoon after one o'clock, what would the cumulative listenership be? Fourteen depressed kids, plus kitchen staff, being forced to listen to a UK import seven-inch by the Buzzcocks. It didn't matter. I liked doing the show, and I got to practice. Because I cared that much. You hope that someone, anyone, besides you and your girlfriend gives a shit about what you're doing. We had no signal, but I acted no differently than if I'd been spinning records at the biggest FM rock station in the tri-state area. I made a few good friends at the "station." Brian Brunden was wearing a Buzzcocks button on the same day I was wearing a Gary Numan T-shirt (that's all it takes, apparently, to become lifelong friends), and we were more or less doing the shows for each other.

The following year, I transferred to Rutgers, and the guy in charge of talent there, Jonathan Schwartz (not the well-known disc jockey and Sinatraphile, but a different DJ who's now on Sirius specializing in jam bands), put me on the air for real.

My shifts at Rutgers varied. Sometimes I was on air from ten at night to two in the morning, or from eight to midnight, which was great. I loved the late-night thing. I was able to play all the synth-punk and new wave and post-punk I wanted. Songs from Human League, Gang of Four, New Order. The Cure when they started out. Romeo Void's "Never Say Never." Then I'd go back and play the eternally cool things that people wanted to hear: Bowie, Iggy, the Velvet Underground. And I really wanted to give local bands a break; that was part of my mission. There was one band I liked called Neighbors and Allies that I used to go see all the time, who never made it, and another band, from Carteret, New Jersey, who had a cool indie EP *Girls about Town*, three original songs with *girl* in the title and a cover of Brian Wilson's "Girl Don't Tell Me." They were the Smithereens, still one of my favorite bands from Jersey, or from anywhere, really.

The first band I ever interviewed on the air—the first time any interview I did went beyond my little corner of Jersey—was a group of Hoboken kids called the Bongos. I heard the band's indie 45 "The Bulrushes" and was captivated. I befriended them and they came up to the station to promote their record. I did it for free because I was such a fan, but that was, I guess you'd say, my official debut as a rock interviewer. I'm still friends with their lead singer and songwriter, Richard Barone, and not long ago I went to the studio where he was recording a new album and taped another one-on-one chat with him, more than thirty years after we met.

I was buying a lot of my records at the Crazy Eddie's record department in East Brunswick, along with a ton of used albums at a New Brunswick store called Cheap Thrills, the store that would get the most imports. A girl who worked at Crazy Eddie's, Maureen, always cut me a discount. "Discount" is understating it. I'd go to the counter with around twenty albums and she'd charge me a couple of dollars. Except for the fact that money changed hands, it was more or less sanctioned shoplifting. I was just a college kid working an overnight security gig, so Maureen really helped me build my record collection. One night I was looking through the import bins and she said, "Listen, I have this friend named Tony Shanahan who's in a great band, the Boogles. You should see them and play them on your show."

"Sure. Where's he playing?"

"Oh, he's at the Melody. It's this cool bar in New Brunswick, by Rutgers."

I met Tony (it turned out his family owned an Irish bakery in Middletown, which was like two miles from where I grew up), and we became friendly. And we still are (he plays bass in Patti Smith's group). The thing about the Melody was, the only music they played between sets was Motown. After the strip club, I'd gotten a DJ job on Tuesday nights at a place in East Brunswick called Charlie's Uncle. It was more a restaurant than a club, tucked away in the middle of a strip mall, but it had a stage area, and I was one of the few "entertainers" it booked. The dinner crowd would be gone early, the kitchen closed down, and at nine it turned into a bar scene. On some nights, the band was a local outfit called Richie Sambora and Friends. That was before Jon Bongiovi and Dave Bryan plucked him from obscurity to help them out on their second album, and we all know what happened after that. Jon's band did all right. I think Charlie's Uncle is now a "happy endings" massage parlor.

The owners designated every Tuesday night as New Wave Night and stuck me up on the stage. I'd have been happier in a DJ booth, where I didn't have to be in the spotlight. Usually, DJs were tucked away somewhere in the back of the club, or up in a booth looking down on the floor, not so conspicuously on display, and I felt awkward when I first walked out and stood there surrounded by milk crates filled with my albums. I was so nervous at the beginning that I got trashed on this horrible blue curacao concoction that we called Janitor in a Drum. I'd pound that crap and play every-thing from new wave—Depeche Mode, Duran Duran—to hits like "Billie Jean." By the time I was into my second song, people were already dancing, and by the third or fourth the floor was filled.

It became the hottest thing to do on a Tuesday night in East Brunswick, not that there was all that much com-petition for your entertainment dollar. Before long, I was drawing three, four hundred people to Charlie's Uncle on

Tuesday nights. I put up flyers, promoted the gig on the radio, and if you wanted to hear new wave music, that was the place you had to go. The word of mouth was incredible.

One night I stopped by the Melody to see Tony, and I asked him who the owners were.

"Those guys over there, Cal and Steve." I went over to them.

"Um, listen. You guys need some updated music. Look, I love Motown as much as the next guy, but there's all this amazing music coming out now." I started hyping them on Elvis Costello and Nick Lowe, the Clash, all this current, vibrant music. At first, they said, "Why don't you make us some tapes?" Sure. I started doing these A-Z Matt Mixes. I made cassettes to play at the club, and every night they played those tapes, people would go downstairs to where the PA was, where the tape player was hooked up, and rip them off. Steal them right out of the deck. We started with about a dozen cassettes, and soon we were down to three. Eventually, Cal and Steve saw what I was doing at Charlie's Uncle, bringing this crowd out to a bar on Route 18 on slow Tuesday nights, and asked me to do that at the Melody. It was a gig that lasted fourteen years.

All of a sudden—this was before the age of club DJs being stars, at least in the non-disco world—I was up on the stage of the Melody with my SL-1200 Technics turntables, playing alt-rock, and at the same time I'm doing a couple of nights a week at the college station. I played current new wave music, and I was also encouraging local acts to give me demos. If I liked them, we'd put the music on carts and I'd spin it on the air.

The Melody became the scene. I did three nights a week, packing it every night. People came from New York City, from Philadelphia, just to hear me spin. It was mostly word of mouth. The club and my radio audience over-lapped somewhat; I'd mention it on the air sometimes, but I didn't have to. Some Rutgers kids came to the Melody, or from other schools nearby, but there were at least as many working-class people, just looking for a night out. I was happy as fuck; I was loving every moment. I was twenty years old, I was getting laid—girls would show up at the club and say, "Hey, I listen to you on the radio," and the next thing I know we're having sex in my car in front of my parents' house—and I'm turning people on to music. What is better than doing everything you want to do? At some point, you're not thinking of it as a jumping-off point to a career, really; you're thinking of it as "This is the best job ever." It was.

I kept my Tuesday gig at Charlie's Uncle for a while (Sambora had almost every other night of the week), moonlighted at other venues, and picked up another couple of nights at a joint called Todd's. I'd be doing three, four shifts a night at different clubs. People would follow me wherever I'd turn up. There were flyers around town: MATT PINFIELD GIVES IT TO YOU FOUR NIGHTS A WEEK, and although one club wouldn't want to promote the others, you'd see that flyer everywhere. I was an in-demand DJ, my girlfriend at the time was making pretty good cash on the tips from the restaurant where she waited tables, I was drinking everywhere for free, and I was finding and sharing music live and on the radio. I'm not sure life could get more ideal than that. I even sang with two local cover bands, the Exceptions and Action, doing my best on songs by Billy Idol and Duran Duran. "Dancing with Myself" and "White Wedding" were staples of my rep-ertoire. I also kept crossing the line with my drinking, and lost my driver's license for around six months after getting pulled over while reeling from the effects of that poison called Long Island iced tea. I was planning on spending that night at a friend's place, which is why I thought I could get away with being hammered, but my friend understandably decided that he would rather have a college girl in his bed than my drunk ass on his sofa.

Like a lot of people with addiction issues, I was mostly oblivious. Sometimes I would black out from drinking, other times I'd be fine, and I didn't see it as anything to be concerned about. What was lucky, or unlucky if you look at it rationally, was that whenever New Jersey changed the legal drinking age, I was always one year on the okay side of the line: I was nineteen when you could drink at eighteen, twenty-two when they upped it to twenty-one. There were never any restrictions, not that it would have mattered to me. I tried every possible cocktail concoction at every club I spun at, people would keep buying me drinks and I kept pounding them, and because alcohol starts bringing your energy down, I tried boosting it with blow or speed. That's how it went during my DJ shifts that lasted six hours on the weekends, from nine p.m. to three a.m.

It was a perfect time to be on college radio, because it was the post-punk era and everyone was going in a hundred different directions, whether it was Echo and the Bunnymen or the Teardrop Explodes, the Cure or the Jam. Some of the new bands were quite unsettling and disturbing, but exhilarating live. Hearing Killing Joke and Bauhaus for the first time—both of their debut albums came out in 1980—was a shock. I had to stand near the back of the club at my first Killing Joke show; I believed they were possessed. The horn sections were using all weird minor chords. The sound was abrasive, heavy, doom and gloom. Where were these guys coming from? They had no precedent. They were grabbing elements of aggressive punk rock, but mixing in shards of speed metal. Sometimes they'd use just a two-word hook, and the tension would mount as the rest of the band followed. I remember thinking: Holy shit, who are these guys? To this day, I think bands like Killing Joke don't get the recognition they deserve. They challenged their audience in the way Rage Against the Machine, Metallica, and Nirvana did later on. They might seem like a footnote, but they didn't give a shit about parameters, they kept advancing.

After Kurt Cobain died, I was driving around with Jaz and Geordie from Killing Joke, talking about how Nirvana basically copped their riff for "Come as You Are" from a song called "Eighties," and Jaz said, "You know, it was hard, our publishing company and our lawyers wanted us to sue them, and they came to us, and we said, Give them a fucking break, let it go. 'Cause, you know, people could say that our song 'Change,' is a lot like War's song 'Me and Baby Brother,' just sped up." So that kind of shit goes on all the time. In 2003, Dave Grohl played drums on Killing Joke's first album in seven years.

On nights when I wasn't spinning, I went with my friends to City Gardens. Whatever was happening that night at that club, we wanted to be a part of it. You felt you were a witness to history. I suppose every generation feels that way. That was our place: a giant warehouse, this big box that drew a punk crowd, a mixture of working-class and college kids. You'd see the same people at every show. To get to the stage, the bands had to walk through the crowd. Then, after the show, the bands went upstairs to an unfinished attic. That's where I met Killing Joke for the first time in 1982.

That same night was also my introduction to rap music. Jaz had a cassette of "The Message" by Grandmaster Flash and the Furious Five, and he popped it into a boom box and said, "This is the best fucking thing out in the world right now." I did not say a single word for the entire song, all seven minutes. *Don't push me 'cause I'm close to the edge.* It all spoke to me: the groove, the words, I'd never heard anything like it. No one had. I thought, This is as punk rock as any of the other shit I listened to: *It's like a jungle sometimes, it makes me wonder how I keep from goin' under.* The junkies, the pissing in the street. That was it for me. I went to the record store the next day and bought the twelve-inch single, and I kept following them, buying every record. *New York, New York, big city of dreams, but everything in New York ain't always what it seems.* Those singles to me were absolutely groundbreaking, and I was in love with them, and fuck the rock fans who can't recognize how connected rock and rap are, how much a group like Public Enemy had in common with rock 'n' roll pioneers like Bo Diddley and Little Richard. Those rap artists are important in advancing the state of rock 'n' roll. It was perfect that it was a band like Killing Joke who opened up that world to me. It was life changing.

Once I made connections at clubs like City Gardens, I got to attend every show for free (except for the first New Order show after Ian Curtis from Joy Division killed himself: that show, at two in the afternoon on a Saturday, was five-dollar admission and no one was comped), and that meant I could spend more money on beer, gas, and records. Those were the essential elements of my college years. And if I was lucky, people who wanted me to play their music on the radio would buy me beers and send me promo copies of records. What could be better than that? All I really needed was gas money.

I couldn't count all the shows I saw at City Gardens: the Replacements, Black Flag, the Circle Jerks, Bauhaus, Thompson Twins, even bands like Men Without Hats and A Flock of Seagulls. At City Gardens, we used to hang out with a young bartender named Jonathan Leibowitz. Years went by, I was at MTV, and I saw Jon Stewart in the hallway. He was doing his first talk show there—this was in 1993, before his run on *The Daily Show*—and I was a fan, so I went up to him and said, "Hey, Jon, I'm Matt. It's great to meet you."

"Matt, what do you mean? You *know* me. It's Jon from City Gardens." I never made the connection. He was the guy behind the bar who was always cool to us, and if a band he liked was onstage, he'd hit the floor to dance, or mosh.

What I was reading about these bands in the mainstream press made me think that the journalists didn't fully get it. You could almost sense their dismay, their ambivalence. I felt these bands were important, so I started bringing my tape recorder with me to every show. It was a crappy old thing with the external mic you had to hold right in front of your interviewee's mouth to get anything audible. I'd go to a show and finagle my way backstage and go, Hey, I'm from the Rutgers station and is it cool if I talk to you for a few minutes? Most of the time they were happy to meet someone who was interested, and then I'd hit them with questions that made it obvious I knew what the fuck I was talking about.

Acts would book shows on the Jersey Shore on the weekends, and none of the local stations would give them air time to promote their gigs. The labels would call us and ask if we'd do an interview. We'd always say, Yeah, bring them down. And that could mean anyone from Trent Reznor and Anthony Kiedis—I did the last Chili Peppers interview before Hillel died of an overdose—to Nick Cave. We let them take over and play whatever records they wanted. It was loose and spontaneous. There was a playlist at the station, but it was so flexible, like: play six to eight of the songs on this list every hour. The rest of the time, it was anything goes. The guests could sit on a stool and play guitar if they wanted. Nowhere else in the area, not in New York or Philly, could you hear Nine Inch Nails or the Chili Peppers.

I would buy imports and independent records by the Gun Club and Dream Syndicate. I was open to finding anything good, and I was discriminating but not elitist. I don't care what anybody says, I love all that '80s synth pop, Adam Ant, Soft Cell, OMD. I played Duran Duran before MTV did, and the first Tears for Fears album.

Once, Bob Weir from the Grateful Dead came in with the jazz drummer Billy Cobham; they'd made an album together, a spinoff thing from the Dead, and I could tell Cobham was thinking, What the fuck is this guy going to know? But I was well informed about the whole jazz-fusion scene. "Billy, I always thought it was criminal that Dreams were the only jazz-rock band on Columbia that didn't make it." And I kept rolling: "Dreams' first album was fantastic, and Doug Lubahn, who played bass on all those Doors albums . . ." And I knew everything about the Mahavishu Orchestra, the sheets-of-sound storm of a band he'd been in with guitarist John McLaughlin and violinist Jerry Goodman from the Flock. Cobham wasn't prepared for any of that; he assumed I was a college kid who wanted to meet the band because I was into the Dead, and I surprised him by switching the topic and focusing on him instead of Weir. All of a sudden, Cobham was totally into the interview. You have to know what you're talking about.

What I was doing on the air was like my version of what I heard on WNEW-FM in New York, which was commercial but also a vestige of real free-form radio, where each DJ's set reflected his (or her, in the case of the Nightbird, Alison Steele) own taste. That's what I wanted my show to be. I keep going back to that desire to proselytize. That was my mission. In my high school yearbook, there's a photo of me outside the school holding a Boomtown Rats record and showing it to two other people, like: You need to know about this. When I discovered Tom Petty or the Clash, it wasn't enough for me to love them for myself. I needed everybody in the world to hear about them. I would be offended when local radio stations deprived their listeners of Aerosmith albums like *Toys in the Attic* and *Get Your Wings*. And if you aren't going to hear Petty and Aerosmith, you sure as hell aren't going to hear Pete Shelley from the Buzzcocks. Or the Specials or the Cure. For a while you could hear those bands mixed in with classic rock like the Eagles and Fleetwood Mac on WPIX in New York, a groundbreaking station, but that bold programming experiment didn't last long enough.

I knew I had to meet the Cure. I'd already seen them live twice, but I had yet to talk to them in person. I found a way to call Chris Perry, the record producer, and I got the number for his UK label, Fiction. I called England from Rutgers—I couldn't very well have charged a call to England on my home phone; my parents would have flipped out—and convinced him to let me do an interview.

What I didn't realize was that I had actually been invited to a press conference. Not even a press conference, really: a room of people sitting around with Robert Smith, the band's lead singer, and the drummer Lol Tolhurst. The questions coming out of these third-tier writers for second-tier papers in a first-tier market (this was promo for a gig in New York Fucking City!) were so uninformed. Ignorant, actually. It was embarrassing.

I could tell that Smith was getting more and more frustrated. The questions kept circling around the somber tones of the music. "Why are you so depressed?" "Have you thought of suicide?" I couldn't believe this. Smith said, trying to keep calm, "Suicide is really tragic to me. To be honest with you, I always think there's a reason to live." He was polite enough, but getting more irritated and agitated.

Once the ordeal was over, Chris Perry went over to Smith and told him I was there to interview him for my college station. He picked up an empty milk carton from the conference room table, crushed it in his hand, and threw it across the room. He was in no mood.

There was a record the Cure were involved with called "I'm a Cult Hero" by Cult Hero, who was the Cure's mailman. The B-side was called "I Dig You," and the lyrics consisted entirely of "I dig you / Do you dig me?" This single, the B-side, had gotten some college radio airplay. I'd spun it a few times at Rutgers. So I went up to Robert Smith and said, "Listen, man, I don't give a fuck about talking about the Cure, but I'd love to talk with you about your mailman."

His face lit up and he said, "Hey, man, how're you doing?" We just started talking. He said one night he and the band were at a pub, and the postman started railing on them, saying, "All you rock 'n' roll bands, you punk bands, you got the good life while I'm out here slogging around delivering the mail." The guys in the Cure told him that if he thought it was so easy, he should go and write a song, and they'd bring him to the studio to record it. That's how this record got made and became a cult underground thing.

We ended up talking for an hour, laughing about the press conference, and we wound up leaving together. It turned into a really fucking fun event that became the start of a long-term relationship with Robert.

Every journalist has the same list of five questions, so I always tried to lead with something different. Otherwise the repetition would make anyone justifiably irritable. In the Radiohead documentary *Meeting People Is Easy*, you can see this fatigue setting in. In one scene, I'm hanging out backstage at Radio City Music Hall with the band, shooting a segment for *120 Minutes*. It's the only time you see Thom Yorke laughing and telling stories. It happened so spontaneously; we had become friendly, and Thom trusted me, so I thought it was going to be a typical interview, updating for the new album, what's going on. When I got to Radio City, I saw Grant Gee, the director of the documentary, and he asked if he could mount a camera on the wall to capture our conversation for his film. What resulted was a moment of light in an otherwise pretty bleak picture of life on the road. People have constantly mentioned the film to me over the years; it's famous for showing how mundane being on the road can be. It's a pretty bleak depiction of the grind, but that one scene made an impression because it's so uncharacteristic. We were talking about the new song "Nude" that hadn't been recorded yet and wouldn't be released for almost another decade, and it's a rare point in the film when Thom lets down his guard and is actually enjoying himself. It's nice to have that preserved on film, the relaxed rapport that Thom and I have had over the years.

Much later, when I first met Chris Martin from Coldplay, the first thing he said when he came up to me was, "You're the guy from the Radiohead movie! The only one Thom likes!" He had no other point of reference for me, he didn't know me from MTV, but he said he could tell I knew my shit and that Thom and I were having fun. I never wanted to be one of those people who became blasé about being around rock stars; I always walked into every situation to have a good time. I have no idea why some interviewers see their role as adversarial, or think that they aren't doing their job if they aren't being provocative or controversial. What's the point?

"Modern Rock on the Jersey Shore"

There was something going on across the country, scattered pockets here and there. Music that was on the fringe was migrating to the center. People started to call it "alternative," and I suppose that's what it was, a counterbalance to the type of polished, predictable rock that the major labels were pumping out. Where there was a vacuum, I created a space at Rutgers, where local bands and music outside the mainstream could get exposure, find an audience. But my reach there was limited, and so were my career options. I wound up staying at college radio even after I wasn't going to college anymore. Where else was I going to go? I got along with my bosses. I knew the market. And the music I programmed dovetailed with my weekly DJ gigs at the Melody. All I wanted to do was stay on the air and play what I considered good music. But I couldn't keep on doing it pro bono, as a public service. It had to lead somewhere.

It led to a private house on a gravel road off Route 18 in Tinton Falls, New Jersey. I'd heard, through my friend Brian, whom I'd bumped into in a New Brunswick record store (so many life-changing moments happened in record stores), that there was a radio station at the Jersey Shore where I'd fit in. I called the station, WHTG, and a guy named Mike Marrone answered the phone. I told him who I was. "Oh,

Matt, I know who you are. I worked at Jem Records and I used to listen to you. You played a lot of good stuff. So you want to be on the air here? Why don't you make us a demo?" I put together something at Rutgers and drove it down to the shore to drop it off in person. WHTG broadcast out of a small roadside house owned by a woman named Faye Gade, who'd bought the station from her father. She still lived there, with her cats, and with the radio staff coming and going.

Faye was eccentric, but so was I, and she gave Rich and Mike the green light to hire me. She also gave me and the other guys on the air the freedom and the ability to run with their own tastes. Even then—especially then, come to think of it—most radio stations made programming decisions based on research, or on what consultants told them to play. I'm not saying all consultants are evil, but the whole system seems full of shit to me. I don't know how a radio consultant who lives in Indiana could tell you what would make a station in the middle of New Jersey connect with its listeners. I don't believe in that, cold-calling people and asking them to listen to twenty-second hooks of songs. Who answers the phone to deal with that? If you're a normal human being who listens to intelligent music, if you have a regular job, a life, and an IQ that cracks three digits, you're not even going to stay on the phone if you get that kind of call. What do consultants know about the pulse of the music? What we were doing at HTG was still considered very fringe. We called it Modern Rock at the Jersey Shore.

It was bare bones, like a garage-band version of professional radio. We were actually bringing in our own records, like at college radio, but with less of a library. I drove down on weekends—my shifts were Saturday and Sunday nights, around six to ten p.m.—and started playing everything I loved. It was my dream playlist, in that it was barely a playlist at all: British imports, new American bands. Julian Cope, Echo and the Bunnymen, New Order. The Smiths were a big one. Bowie, Lou Reed. Deep Beatles tracks, Elvis Costello. I might throw in the Byrds' "I'll Feel a Whole Lot Better." It was so diverse.

The interesting thing was, even though we were on the Jersey Shore, which of course is Springsteen country, the station didn't want us to play Bruce, because that was around the time he exploded everywhere with *Born in the U.S.A.* and was on every AOR and Top 40 station nonstop. So in order to distinguish ourselves, we didn't play his most popular stuff. I mean, Bruce loved the station, he told me later on, and I always played his deeper album cuts and tracks from *Greetings from Asbury Park, N.J.* and *Nebraska*. WNEW, the big New York City rock station, still owned Memorial Day weekend on the boardwalk in Asbury Park. That was their turf, the whole South Jersey scene, so we mostly avoided it. I like a lot of those guys, Southside Johnny, the Iron City Houserockers, but we were into a whole different thing. We were more of the City Gardens/Fast Lane gang, although there was some overlap. Bruce would show up at the Fast Lane, for example, to play "Fever" with the Stray Cats. It wasn't really a rivalry, but the audiences were from different factions. On one side you have the traditional bar-band ethos that the E Street Band and the Jukes were born out of, and on the other, the more modern, adventurous stuff. Like U2, when they first hit Jersey—they were a Fast Lane band.

At that time there were so few commercial stations doing what HTG was doing. Maybe thirteen scattered across America. Things changed slowly. We were located midway between the major markets of Philadelphia and New York City, and bands making their way up or down between gigs in those cities—or who booked weekend dates on the shore—would stop by, because we were the only game in town. We were playing Nine Inch Nails and the Red Hot Chili Peppers. Hillel Slovak and Anthony Kiedis from the Peppers pulled up that dirt driveway in an RV and came in for an interview while Flea stayed behind sleeping in the van. Trent Reznor came in. For years, well into the '90s, we were the one stop every alternative act had to make. My thing was to always let the guests take over, like Nick Cave or Jeff Buckley, let them play records that mattered to them, or sit on a stool and play guitar. Do whatever they wanted to do. It was really loose and spontaneous. There was a playlist, sort of, but it was written on index cards (we couldn't afford a computer) and was along the lines of "play two of these artists per hour." Beyond that, no guidelines.

Except when it came to sexual lyric content. We had carte blanche in most areas, but Faye wanted to keep the music clean. Once she freaked out about some words in "Good Stuff" by the B-52's, which isn't even that rude, but she wanted it taken off the air. We never could have gotten away with playing Prince's more explicit songs, so there was a bit of self-censorship going on because we didn't want to get in trouble, but that seemed like a decent trade-off to me, if that was the only thing we'd get busted for. Although I'm sure we played Berlin's "Sex" at certain times and I never got any crap about that one. In terms of genre, or just stylistically, we played whatever we wanted.

Radio is a weird place to work. You get the crazies who

come out. One woman grabbed me one night as I was leaving the station, pulled me on top of a car, and said, "If you don't fuck me, my friends are bikers, I'm going to have them come here and kill you." That scared the shit out of me, and I knew I'd have to fast-talk my way out of it, because what would the police do? I got insane fan mail, people sending blood-stained letters, a woman who said she rubbed the letter on her pussy and wrote SMELL THIS. Psychotic shit. You didn't know how far these women were going to go. And someone could accuse you of something that you didn't even do. (Not that I was that well behaved: I once got a blow job while I was on the air, and got laid in the station's record library. There are perils, and then there are perks.)

There was a girl who came to the Melody once in a while who approached me one night. Her name was Monica and she was about to graduate from Rutgers, had seen me spin at the club and heard me on the radio, and she asked if she could hire me to be the DJ at her graduation party. I said sure and forgot all about it, and one day she showed up at the station and asked, "Are you going to do this or not?" I DJed the party, and right after that she and I started seeing each other. I shared a summer house with a bunch of friends down the shore on Long Beach Island, and she'd come and stay there. By January we were living together, and she found out she was pregnant. She told me over dinner and said, "I think we can do this," and I agreed, but I was pretty shell-shocked. I'd had a lot of espresso at the restaurant and was keyed up anyway, and I spent much of the night in a rocking chair thinking, Oh, shit, here comes real life. It was like a Springsteen song. In April we got married, and our daughter Jessica was born on September 12, 1986. Monica and I were watching a Beatles documentary when her contractions started, and when I called the doctor he said we'd better get to St. Peter's Hospital right away.

After watching Monica give birth and holding Jessica for the first time, I called HTG to tell them the news and to ask whoever was on the air if he would play David Bowie's "Kooks," a song on *Hunky Dory* that he wrote about the birth of his son Zowie. As I drove home from the hospital that night, I heard the song on the radio, Bowie singing, "Soon you'll grow so take a chance / With a couple of kooks hung up on romancing." It's a great, honest tune all about going on the adventure of becoming a new dad. You might not be ready, but you leap in.

I got a cassette in the mail one day at the station with a letter that said, We're an original band, listen to our music, the usual pitch. I got in my car to drive back to South Brunswick and I put this tape in and I hear this ranting and raving, no music at all, and it dawns on me that I'm listening to a recording of the mass suicide at Jonestown, people screaming, dying, while Jim Jones is going on this amphetamine rant. Someone had put forty-five minutes of this on a cassette just to fuck with me.

The American band that changed everything was R.E.M. They were the template for what started to be called "alternative," and from this vantage point, four decades later, when they're still considered one of the all-time great rock bands of any genre, it's important to remember how radical they sounded, like they were beaming in from a radio station that wasn't quite tuned in right: they were like a magical blur of sound, everything—Michael Stipe's vocals, Peter Buck's guitar tones—designed to make you move in closer to catch it all. Almost everything on the radio then was sharp and crisp, and this was music that was anything but. They brought mystery back.

One night I was at Maxwell's, the famous now-shuttered Hoboken rock club, and my old friend Richard Barone from the Bongos came up to me and said, "Listen, we know you were from Athens, Georgia, before you moved up here, and we told this Athens band that opened for us how cool you are, and they said to make sure to give you a copy of their single." It was the seven-inch of R.E.M.'s "Radio Free Europe" and "Sitting Still" on Hib-Tone. I loved the A-side but, as usual, I was hooked even more by the flip side, how melancholy it was. Even if you didn't understand everything Michael was singing, it was pure emotion.

By the time I got to HTG in '84, R.E.M. was probably the number-one alternative rock band in the US, with tracks like "So. Central Rain (I'm Sorry)," "(Don't Go Back to) Rockville," and "Can't Get There from Here," all on I.R.S. Records. We played them constantly, along with the Cure, Depeche Mode, Dramarama, Lloyd Cole and the Commotions. The Commotions' *Rattlesnakes* is one of my favorite albums ever. Years later, I was hanging out with the guys from Fountains of Wayne—another great Jersey band—and they mentioned that they were going to hang out with Lloyd Cole, the lead singer of the Commotions, later on.

"Guys, you have to fucking call him. Ask him to come meet us."

Lloyd showed up and of course I went into hyperfan mode: "Lloyd, man, I love that lyric, 'Must you tell me all your secrets when it's hard enough to love you knowing nothing.'"

"What song is that from?"

It was from "Four Flights Up," a song on *Rattlesnakes*. That's a thing I've encountered time after time: knowing an artist's music so thoroughly, being so deep into it, that I end up quoting lyrics back to them that they don't even remember writing. Or mentioning that someone played keyboards on some track on an early album, and the artist says, "I didn't know that." On their own album.

Lloyd Cole and the Commotions, Dramarama—people might not know them as well as they know bands like R.E.M. and the Cure. But they were so important to the format; they were artists that distinguished us. Dramarama is considered an LA band, but they got their start in Wayne, New Jersey. They were friends of mine, and even though Rodney Bingenheimer on K-Rock in Los Angeles is credited with breaking the band, we were actually playing them earlier at WHTG. The guys in the band owned a record store in New Jersey, and I was playing them as a local band before the label New Rose picked them up. In that format, "Anything, Anything" was a classic, maybe the biggest alternative record on the West Coast until "Smells Like Teen Spirit." It was that influential, and I'm one of a handful of people thanked on their album *Cinéma Vérité*.

There was definitely a movement building with the American indie bands; the English synth bands like Blancmange, OMD, Tears for Fears, who kind of lived in both worlds, mainstream and alternative; even pop-alternative bands like Thompson Twins and A Flock of Seagulls. It was a strange moment, part synth, part new wave, part new romantic, part power pop like Squeeze, part goth, part kudzu rock like R.E.M., and HTG was one of the pioneering radio stations in what became, ultimately, a dominant stream. Having that platform was a major deal, and as the station's influence built, I eventually was given the gig as the station's music director, which meant that I was one of two people making all the programming decisions, and the landscape started to change for me.

I have to give Faye a lot of credit for my promotion. She hired Michael Butcher from WHSF in Washington, DC, another one of the first thirteen or so original alternative stations, to be the station's program director, and he was considering someone else for music director. She told him that before he made his final decision, he should meet with me. Not only did I end up doing five days a week on the air, but I also got the music director position. That's what kicked the door down: people in the music business, other radio programmers, promo reps, record executives, the people at MTV all discovered who I was.

What I gathered from the people that I met in the industry was that my enthusiasm was a breath of fresh air. I was looking for reasons to play records, not to *not* play them. There were so few places to get new things heard and to get your foot in the door in major markets. Especially growing up between New York and Philly, where it's not as easy to just roll into a radio station and ask for the mic.

We had to create a new niche in between these markets. The record labels saw the opportunity and started departments devoted to the promotion and marketing of alternative music. That had never really existed before. There was rock radio, and pop radio, and artists fit—or were made to fit—into either of those formats. And there was college radio, which started gaining more influence in the early '80s with the *CMJ (College Media Journal) New Music Report*, which tracked airplay for college and noncommercial stations. But starting in the mid-'80s, the labels had no choice; they had to jump into the boat or drown.

You could feel the ground shifting. The dominance of the hair-band era, when labels were signing the second- and third-tier hard rock bands, was starting to wane, the way it always happens near the end of any musical cycle. What was cool gets repeated and repeated and becomes a parody of itself to the point where it's hard to get excited about the next band sticking to the same formula. When Guns N' Roses' *Appetite for Destruction* came out in '87, people unfairly lumped them in with the other hair-metal bands, even though they were coming from another place. I know Guns N' Roses never considered themselves part of that Sunset Strip/Club Lingerie community, really. Although the band was influential in that world, kids who were into grimier punk rock were paying attention also. The thing about Guns was that they brought some of that punk attitude with them. Some of their songs sounded like Dead Boys songs to me. It was just gritty and nasty enough. I remember seeing them after *Appetite* came out, at an invite-only gig at the Ritz on Eleventh Street in New York, standing next to Thurston Moore from Sonic Youth. I'm pretty sure if it had been a band like Warrant or Slaughter, Thurston wouldn't have felt compelled to check it out. Guns were something else.

HTG already had an incredibly proactive audience. But now all of a sudden it was like people were coming in from everywhere. Our ratings continued to grow. Monmouth in Ocean County was a medium-size market in the shadow of New York and Philadelphia, but to people in the music and radio business, we really mattered. Bands made it a point to visit us, and it was hilarious the way the British bands, in particular, who grew up in Manchester, Liverpool,

Birmingham, wherever, would have this idea in their heads about what it would be like to Come to America. It was this grandiose notion based on what they knew from the movies, or seeing footage of groups like the Beatles landing at JFK. Instead they've wound up in this little house in the middle of Noplace, New Jersey. That was part of the game. They have to make all these stops across the country, play out-of-the-way gigs, be interviewed on alternative radio stations. I'm sure we must have seemed like a joke to some of them, but our influence far exceeded our size.

It wasn't until 1989 that I had the chance to go to England. It was mythical to me. The birthplace of the Beatles and the Stones, the Jam and the Clash. Everything I knew about the country I knew from films and song lyrics. I'd made friends with Miles Hunt, the lead singer of the Wonder Stuff, one of those bands who had UK success but never broke through in the US. He told me to book the trip and meet them in Brighton, and then he'd include me in the tour rider as someone on the band's payroll. My flight was canceled, and if I didn't get to Brighton, I'd miss the tour. But I managed to jump onto an overnight flight and then a bus to Brighton, and I felt like I was finally connecting in person with the England of my imagination. Brighton, home to the famous fracas between the mods and rockers that Pete Townshend wrote about in *Quadrophenia*. The place that inspired "Rumble in Brighton" by the Stray Cats, and "Brighton Rock" by Queen, where you can hear the sounds of the amusement park on the pier. Brighton was also the setting of the UK rock movie *That'll Be the Day* with David Essex and Ringo Starr. I was so immersed in the history of this place, and in all of London too. I went back to London with the band and explored that city for the first time, seeing sites I'd heard sung about on records when I was a kid: "Sunny South Kensington" by Donovan. St. John's Wood, which I'd only known as someplace the Stones mentioned in "Play with Fire."

"Oh, my God," I thought. "All the songs are coming to life!"

It was a dream fulfilled, to be walking those streets that had been immortalized on the records. Since then, I've been to England so many times, with so many bands, but as amazing as those experiences were, I'll always be grateful to Miles, who gave me that first mind-blowing experience.

When I took over as HTG's music director, we were sitting at the epicenter of the biggest seismic upheaval rock music had seen in nearly three decades. I got the gig in 1990, and sometimes you're the beneficiary of perfect timing. WHTG was like one of the original colonies that became the United States of America. From a small private house, a station stuck between two major markets, history was being made. I remember going to my first Gavin radio convention. The *Gavin Report* was a music industry tip sheet, telling radio programmers what was new every week, what records they should be watching or playing. It was part of the free-spending, incestuous relationship between the radio side of the business and the record companies: labels took out ads in the *Gavin Report* to plug their music and sent artists to play at the annual convention. Advertising and promo appearances replaced the envelopes of $50 bills that might have passed between promotion guys and disc jockeys back in the 1950s.

The convention at the Westin Hotel in San Francisco was a circus of debauchery. Free booze, free lodging, rock 'n' roll, and all the accessories that come along with it. That's when the music business still had money to throw around. It's a giant schmoozefest. Michael, my program director, and I were there, being plied with liquor and food. We were all sloshed and stuffed for the evening showcases. (There were shows in the afternoon as well: the first time I ever saw Eminem was in a cafeteria at a Gavin convention, doing "My Name Is" while people gorged themselves at the free buffet, barely paying attention.) We were taken to a showcase in a pool hall to see an unknown band called Mookie Blaylock, who were the new edition of Mother Love Bone. There was a handwritten poster taped to the wall: MOOKIE BLAYLOCK (FORMERLY MOTHER LOVE BONE) 9:00. Within a year, they changed their name to Pearl Jam. I wish I'd saved that flyer.

Later on, there was another band, I don't remember their name, but they were essentially like a Police tribute band, only with bad original songs, so I wasn't into it. We split, and the next thing I remembered was being on the floor of my hotel room with my head on a pillow and no pants on. I was told that a girl from a record label had gone back to my room with me, but by that point she was gone, if she had even been there at all. This was all on my first night in San Francisco. Michael came back into the room, saw me, and said, "Matt, I think you should turn over." Because I was just lying there on my back with my dick out. At one point, apparently I'd been pissing out the window. I saw everything at that convention: women with giant dildos, tables filled with cocaine.

Not surprisingly, this period of indulgence led, as it does, to my initial stint in rehab. I went to Faye one day at the station and told her I'd decided to get help. It wasn't one major moment that led me to that decision, it was an accumulation of incidents over the years, because alcoholism and addiction have their effect on people you love and work with, anybody close to you. As the saying goes, when a dog gets wet and it shakes the water off, nobody walks away dry: everyone gets affected. The reality was, the signs had been there for a long time. I was still spinning three or four nights a week in clubs, still DJing at weddings and parties (HTG, for all its influence, was in a secondary market and didn't pay all that well, so I always needed extra cash), drinking at every gig and every event, and what it came down to was, I have to get a grip on this situation. I checked into a facility in New York City that's still one of the roughest places I've ever been. Half the people who were there were not there voluntarily: they'd gotten busted for selling or for possession, and rehab was court-mandated. But I powered through the program and it helped me get control, for a while.

Beyond taking advantage of all the recreational opportunities that came in the package of being in the rock-music community in the early '90s, we took our role in the culture seriously as hell.

We were maybe a dozen trendsetting radio stations, programmed by people who loved the music and were giving underexposed bands a platform. We felt privileged and special, and we knew we were making a difference. At the time, alternative radio was wide open. You could play cool hip-hop, jazz-influenced things like Us3, anything that made sense to us. The funny thing is, I love so many things about classic rock. Those records are part of my DNA. But I felt as though I was part of the revolution, as corny as that sounds. Radio, mainstream rock radio, was very stagnant, and metal was getting repetitive and unimaginative. We were providing the counterpoint, and all that was missing was the one breakthrough band. Once that band came along, everything would change.

For two years in a row, 1992 and 1993, I was named Music Director of the Year, which is a very big deal for someone who was at a small station based on a fucking dirt road in the middle of Jersey. I'm proud of that, but I think in a lot of ways what made that happen was that the music caught up with us.

It was absolutely brewing. I saw it every night when I DJed at a club, or went to see a show at City Gardens. People were there to hang out and be a part of something new. At that time, the alternative and college departments were like the ragtag misfits at the labels, working to get attention for bands who would sell maybe thirty thousand albums, bands who had a cult following, enough to not lose money on them and give the label some rock credibility. I was working seven days a week and putting all my energy into it because I was excited to be in a position where I was making decisions about the music being played. I knew I had an audience.

We were a small platoon of renegade radio, and we all looked at what the others were playing, because we didn't want to miss out. It might have been a local record out of San Diego or Chicago, or something catching fire in Seattle. We needed to know about it so we could decide if it would work for us. Little did we know, in 1990, what was right around the corner, how much it was going to affect every one of our lives. Change the music industry. Change the face of rock.

50 ESSENTIAL ROCK ALBUMS:
THE '80s

Beastie Boys—*Paul's Boutique*

Black Flag—*Damaged*

The Bongos—*Drums Along the Hudson*

David Bowie—*Scary Monsters (and Super Creeps)*

Lloyd Cole and the Commotions—*Rattlesnakes*

Elvis Costello—*Imperial Bedroom*

The Cult—*Love*

The Cure—*Standing on a Beach*

Depeche Mode—*Music for the Masses*

Descendents—*Milo Goes to College*

Dramarama—*Cinéma Vérité*

Duran Duran—*Rio*

Echo and the Bunnymen—*Ocean Rain*

The English Beat—*I Just Can't Stop It*

Faith No More—*The Real Thing*

Peter Gabriel—*Melt*

The Gun Club—*Fire of Love*

Guns N' Roses—*Appetite for Destruction*

Hüsker Dü—*Zen Arcade*

Jane's Addiction—*Nothing's Shocking*

The Jesus and Mary Chain—*Darklands*

Joy Division—*Substance*

Killing Joke—*Debut/What's THIS For . . . !* (Double Disc)

Metallica—*Master of Puppets*

Mötley Crüe—*Dr. Feelgood*

New Order—*Substance*

Nine Inch Nails—*Pretty Hate Machine*

Pixies—*Doolittle*

Tom Petty—*Full Moon Fever*

The Pogues—*If I Should Fall from Grace with God*

Pretenders

Prince—*Purple Rain*

Psychedelic Furs—*Talk Talk Talk*

Lou Reed—*New York*

R.E.M.—*Murmur*

The Replacements—*Let It Be*

Siouxsie and the Banshees—*Once Upon a Time: The Singles*

Slayer—*Reign in Blood*

The Smithereens—*Especially for You*

The Smiths—*The Queen Is Dead*

Squeeze—*Singles—45's and Under*

Sonic Youth—*Daydream Nation*

The Sound—*From the Lions Mouth*

The Stone Roses

Tears for Fears—*The Hurting*

U2—*Boy*

Violent Femmes

The Waterboys—*This Is the Sea*

The Wonder Stuff—*The Eight Legged Groove Machine*

X—*Wild Gift*

The Great Northwest:
How Nirvana Saved the World

Me and the Foo Fighters

In the '60s, the Northwest gave us the Sonics, Paul Revere and the Raiders, and the Kingsmen, bands who made stomping, noisy, unbridled garage rock: "The Witch," "Strychnine," "Like, Long Hair," and "Louie Louie." There was something defiantly sloppy about those records, like the damp Northwest weather got into the grooves of the 45s. The Kingsmen's version of "Louie Louie" sounds as though it was recorded in a flooded basement. It was the grimiest pop record ever to top the charts, until "Smells Like Teen Spirit."

Here's how I see it: being at WHTG during the whole Northwest explosion was like I imagine it must have felt to be at a Top 40 station, WMCA or WABC, in early 1964 when the Beatles shattered the format. It was that kind of moment where you're lucky to be sitting in front of a microphone, having an audience, and being part of a cultural sea change. You can't imagine the rush of being one of the people who helps kick-start that. I'd felt something similar at Rutgers; I knew we were exploring new territory, but we were still a ragtag renegade outfit of musical misfits. Commercially, the mid-'80s belonged to the mainstream—Madonna, Prince, Michael Jackson, Bruce Springsteen, Lionel Richie—and when people started using the word *alternative*, that's what they meant: a counterbalance, a less-traveled road. But what happens when the band of outsiders becomes the rock establishment?

I kept meeting English bands like the Wonder Stuff, who would mention bands like Tad, Mudhoney, and Nirvana, and I'd read about those then-obscure US bands in British magazines like *Sounds*, *Melody Maker*, and the *NME*. So something was up, and naturally I had to find out what was causing this murmur. I bought the *Bleach* album by Nirvana on Sub Pop Records, and immediately I thought how cool the harmonies were on "About a Girl," and how hip they must be to do a Shocking Blue cover, "Love Buzz." That fascinated me. Then the label sent me the "Sliver" single at the station, and I remember saying to Michael, the program director, "Listen, I want to add this record. There's something going on with this band. I loved their last record, but this one is so fucking cool. Let me start it in medium rotation, and if we get some reaction, we can bump it to heavy for a little while." We weren't being hyped on the band or the record by the label; all they did was mail me the single. But I just had a feeling about this one. I was excited by it.

It was quick. It was simple. It had a memorable chorus. The melody was poppy and the lyric was relatable, but it was distorted, crunchy, sloppy, and nasty, and I loved that it had all those different things going on. So Michael let me day-part it, only after five in the afternoon and late at night. But pretty soon we moved it up and started playing it from noon through the whole night. We were one of the few stations in America that officially had "Sliver" on our playlist. It was this instinctive inkling that I had, that Nirvana was something different, and I'd testify to that by programming them for my audience.

Pretty soon, the calls started coming in: "Hey, how fucking cool that you're playing Nirvana. I never thought I'd hear them on the radio." That's the response I got. I'm sure some other people had no idea what the fuck was going on, because Nirvana sure didn't sound like anything else on the station, but later on it was obvious that being early on that band had a lot to do with the success of the station. It was clear to some of us that Nirvana was going to get signed to a major label, but no one, not us, not the label that signed them—DGC—or their management, and certainly not the guys in the band had any idea how everything was going to change. They were just another promising indie band taking the next logical career step. They wanted to be on the same label as Sonic Youth and maybe sell fifty thousand copies of their major-label debut. That would've been considered a real achievement, fifty thousand albums sold.

I remember the day in '91 when "Smells Like Teen Spirit" arrived at the station, a CD single and a seven-inch promo vinyl single that I still have in my living room. That 45 is such a cool thing to have: it signifies the individuality of the song, the power of the single, how much musical and cultural power can be contained in five minutes. How five minutes can shake the world.

We added the record immediately. I was one of the first people to play it, certainly on the East Coast, and across the country maybe there were ten of us who were putting it on the air and getting calls: "What is *that*?" It was as shocking, fresh, and subversive as "I Want to Hold Your Hand" or "Like a Rolling Stone" were. For a while, it was like belonging to a secret society. Not for long.

One night a few days later, I was in the city at CBGB's, and everyone on the sidewalk was talking about that record, trying to reconstruct the lyrics, figuring out what it meant, not just as a song, but what it meant existentially. When Samuel Bayer made the video, the game was over. That clip of that song changed everybody's perception, changed what kids thought was cool. Like that. And all across the country, a thousand hair-metal bands were thinking, Uh-oh, we are FUCKED. Because even though some of those bands were still having hits, it was already starting to feel like the tail end of the heyday. The era that had started with Quiet Riot's cover of Slade's "Cum On Feel the Noize"—a record that the band's lead singer didn't even want to cut—and continued with bands like Ratt, Winger, and Cinderella suddenly felt musty and dated. In the movie *The Wrestler*, Mickey Rourke's character says, "That Kurt Cobain guy really fucked everything up." To this day, people who love '80s hair metal basically feel that was the beginning of the end. Nirvana was the anti-Warrant.

The guys in Nirvana, and the other Northwest bands, saw how rock was being promoted during the entire period of the hair-metal thing and didn't want to be associated with it. They wanted to distance themselves from the clichés.

It was like in the '60s, when bands in the Bay Area—the Airplane, the Dead, Quicksilver, Big Brother—drew a line between themselves and the bands down in Los Angeles. In both instances there was an attitude of "That's not us." The outsiders eventually took over.

It was everywhere, even in the go-go bars, and when I would put it on at the Melody, people would just go berserk: the song would start and catch fire, with Grohl's fucking insane drum intro, and that iconic guitar riff, and the place exploded, like a collective orgasm. I'd never witnessed anything like that, how intensely everyone embraced it. And in a way, it was a validation of everything I stood for. The alternative scene was where I'd set up camp and staked my claim; it was the music I played at every club I'd ever DJed in, at Rutgers, at HTG. When R.E.M. broke through, we were still very much a fringe format, but when Nirvana came along, everybody stood up and took notice, every label wanted to get into the alternative game, and every Seattle band got signed to a major.

I got a call from Mark Kates at Nirvana's label. "Matt, listen, since you're one of the first people who ever believed in Nirvana and played them on the radio, why don't you come hang with us and watch them rehearse for *Saturday Night Live*?" This was in January of '92. So it was Mark, my friend Cliff, and me onstage as the band ran through "Teen Spirit" and "Territorial Pissings," a private audience with what was now the most significant rock band in the US. Afterward, we talked a little. It was happening so fast and they were just trying to be themselves, stay on the ground, not lose sight of who they were. That's what I gathered from everything I witnessed that day, and from the conversation. Kurt had a great sense of humor, and he and the guys were busting each other's balls on the stage, fucking around, because they had to keep that insular thing. It's vital when you're being bombarded from every angle and meeting people like radio guys from New Jersey. It must all become a blur after a while.

It was like what Peter Frampton told me, about when he became so incredibly popular with *Frampton Comes Alive!* He got sick of his own music and would turn it off. He said, "Bowie once said, it's like being strapped to a rocket, and all of a sudden you're in the stratosphere and you're all by yourself. At least the Beatles had each other." For a while, that worked out okay for Nirvana; they had each other, almost all the way up until the end. Kurt had all those issues with drugs, with stomach problems. There were a lot of things going on. And being called the Spokesman of Your Generation when you maybe don't want that pressure—did Dylan even want it?

Krist Novoselic, Nirvana's bass player, told me, "On one hand, Kurt loved it and really wanted to be the biggest star in the world, and on the other hand, he didn't want the responsibility." It was part of the punk rock ethic, growing up in that punk rock community where you're not supposed to care, but you've formed this band and you definitely want people to hear it, and once the music is out in the world, you have no control over who it reaches, who your fans are. Especially when it hits as hard and fast as Nirvana did.

I developed a good rapport with the Seattle guys, including Alice in Chains, Soundgarden, all of them. Little gestures of trust, endorsements from the musicians who were skeptical of everything and everybody. Soundgarden would fly me up to Seattle to interview them, and put me up at the famous—infamous, really—Edgewater Inn, the first place the Beatles stayed when they visited Seattle, the hotel that was the scene of the notorious Led Zeppelin mud shark story, and where Keith Moon from the Who was fishing out the window into Puget Sound. They should have plaques outside the rooms of that joint: KEITH MOON FISHED HERE; JOHN LENNON SLEPT HERE; MEMBERS OF LED ZEPPELIN ENGAGED IN UNSPEAKABLE ACTS HERE. I went over to Kim Thayil's house (he was the lead guitarist in Soundgarden) and hung out in his basement; he had this amazing collection of punk rock records and a classic tube radio from the 1930s.

Years later, we got together with a bunch of guys at a diner. The TV was tuned to MTV; it's Sunday night, so there I am on the screen, and they all started busting my balls. It wasn't like I was some industry talking head; they always treated me like they appreciated where I was coming from, and I have to say, being in the center of that explosion, it was like being someone like Alan Freed in the early days of rock 'n' roll, or Murray the K when he was calling himself the Fifth Beatle. I gave them the respect they deserved, and they gave me credibility.

Nirvana blew the doors off the hinges, but they didn't come out of nowhere, and they weren't alone. Up and down the West Coast, bands had been shaking up the rock scene, and I was open to anything that was causing commotion. In 1987, I opened my first package from Sub Pop. It grabbed my attention because I thought the name of the label was cool. The EP, called *Screaming Life* (again, a very cool title: they were already two for two), contained six songs by a band

I hadn't heard of called Soundgarden. I thought, Well, this looks intriguing to me. The artwork, the look of the band, the title of the lead track, "Hunted Down." They weren't trying to fit in; they were doing their own thing. Some songs I liked immediately. But they were still a young band working at finding themselves.

Their first full-length album, *Ultramega OK*, came out a year later, and it was obvious on tracks like "Flower" that they were really coming into their own. They covered Howlin' Wolf's "Smokestack Lightning," which was like something all the '60s British rock and blues bands would do. It felt like a torch-passing thing, a return to UK groups like the Stones, the Yardbirds, and the Animals, who worshipped American blues. A sense of history always carries a lot of weight with me. Chris Cornell played off hard rock and metal clichés and classic sex-song tropes, offering a kind of sonic commentary; it felt very self-aware to me. The song "Big Dumb Sex" from their next LP, *Louder Than Love*, summed up a lot of what was already becoming stale. It pointed back toward bands like Led Zeppelin and forward to what would define the Seattle sound.

You've got to look at where we were at that time, what the predominant rock vibe was. In '87, Bon Jovi had taken over the world with "Livin' on a Prayer." You have to give it up for those guys; they've worked harder than anyone, and they earned every bit of their success, but that was the sound of mainstream rock then. And Aerosmith's *Permanent Vacation*, an incredible rock album, right in the pocket, but pretty slick. R.E.M. was still the marquee band for the alternative music scene at that time, and that's the world that existed in modern rock when bands like Soundgarden and Jane's Addiction were coming up. They were divisive bands, even within the alternative rock community. If you're a guy like Dave Faulkner, who was in an Australian power-pop group I loved, Hoodoo Gurus, and you're coming from the more power-pop side of the alternative scene, you'd hear something like Jane's Addiction and simply hate it. It was like the polar opposite, but that's where things were heading. Soundgarden's *Badmotorfinger*, Nirvana's *Nevermind*, Pearl Jam's *Ten* all coming within a few months of each other in 1991: that was when everything turned completely upside down, but the seeds of the revolution were planted as a response to the formulaic rock of the mid-to-late '80s. Nirvana's "Love Buzz" and Soundgarden's "Flower" in '89, Alice in Chains' "We Die Young" in '90—those were the first bulletins we received before the takeover.

One afternoon, I was standing outside the HTG house and a white van pulled up into the stone driveway. A guy came out; he looked like a hundred other Jersey rock guys. "Hey, I'm Dean DeLeo. Remember me?" I didn't, really, but he told me he used to see me around at shows on the shore. "Look, man, I live in San Diego now, but I'm back to see my mom. My brother Robert and I started this band." I'm just friendly; I'm very welcoming to people. Be open, help out a musician. Dean explained that he was the guitarist, his brother Robert was on bass, and the lead singer was a guy they'd met out in California named Scott Weiland. They'd just gotten a record deal with Atlantic and had cut their first album. The band was called Stone Temple Pilots, and the album was *Core*. I told him Atlantic wasn't even promoting the album yet; at least I hadn't been hyped on it, but our station was the logical place to go. Dean went back to the van and got a CD (this was back when CDs still came in the cardboard long box) and asked me if I'd give it a listen. We went into the studio, and all I asked him was if there was any language on the songs that I should worry about, any words or references that might get me or the station in trouble, and when he told me it was all clear, I told him I'd play the record on the air. I didn't bother to prescreen it. The first cut I played on the radio—for all I know, and it's certainly possible, it was the first time STP was played on the radio anywhere on the planet—was the track "Wicked Garden."

Now I guess that at the time, when they started to break, some people were calling STP derivative, or a commercialization of grunge (which is hilarious, considering that that was the most commercially successful rock sound of the early '90s by far), but all I heard was the enormous power of what they were doing. It was the initial first album produced by Brendan O'Brien, who was an engineer on the great Red Hot Chili Peppers album *Blood Sugar Sex Magik* and on two albums from 1992 that I loved: the Black Crowes' *The Southern Harmony and Musical Companion* and the Jayhawks' *Hollywood Town Hall*. Brendan's production on *Core* was so dynamic, the textures so visceral and compelling, and he went on to produce Pearl Jam's *Vs.*, Rage Against the Machine, Springsteen's *The Rising*, and so many other classic albums. *Core* was an incredible debut, with tracks like "Sex Type Thing" and "Plush," but on that day Dean pulled up into the HTG driveway, he was just another local guy hustling to get anyone to pay attention. Within months, STP was becoming one of the biggest bands in America. "Plush" was released as the second single, the band did an unplugged version of the song for MTV's *Headbangers Ball*, and DJs—including me at HTG—started playing that version on the air.

Atlantic called me and told me how happy the band was that I took a shot on them. Dean wanted to come by the studio. At that point they were in demand everywhere and could have easily skipped a trip to our station, but Dean dropped in and we joked about how "Plush" was going to be the biggest hit of the summer of '93 (it ended up winning the band a Grammy for Best Hard Rock Performance).

When the second album, *Purple*, was about to come out, the band invited me down to Atlanta to hear it. It was the one with "Interstate Love Song" and "Vaseline." They played a show where the opening acts were the Butthole Surfers and the Meat Puppets, and it was a wild night. That was the first time I met Scott Weiland, and the cracks were already showing. I recognize behavior that was on the brink, and I don't think his drug use had completely gotten the best of him yet, but it was getting there. Not when he was onstage. Onstage, he was fucking great. But it was no shock to me when, in between albums two and three, he was arrested for drug possession.

I was flown out to Los Angeles for a press conference, broadcast live on over three hundred radio stations, announcing that Scott was getting out of rehab. That's what a huge deal that was, and the band was trying to be cool and understanding through the whole ordeal, but I could tell that Dean was pissed. He was not as forgiving. I get it: you reach a level that 99.9 percent of rock bands can only fantasize about. You're selling millions of albums on your first two releases, and the lead singer fucks up in such a major way. It puts the whole thing in jeopardy. Your whole career, your whole life.

I'm the last person on the planet who's in a position to judge. These guys were in the grip of something that they didn't understand and couldn't control. You look at Kurt and Scott, and Layne, and Andrew Wood from Mother Love

Bone, and you see the level of anguish and despair in their lives, how it's manifest in the music. I think a lot of times, especially as the front man of a band, music can help make creative sense out of the baggage you're carrying around, often from a very, very young age, whether it's molestation or neglect or abuse. You're living that shit out loud every night onstage singing those songs. For some people its cathartic, for others it brings up all the rage that you can't quell with anything except heroin. That music was dark and came from a deeper place than the hair metal that had proceeded it, where it was all about hedonistic impulses and partying and getting laid. It's still so shocking to me that bands like Nirvana, Pearl Jam, Alice in Chains, Soundgarden, and STP were able to come along and make such an impact, and I think it shocked them also.

You start a rock band, you want people to hear you, as many people as possible, ideally, because as much as you loved the bands who didn't "make it"—the Melvins, Green River, the Gun Club—there's that part of you that wants to be the Stones or Led Zeppelin. You can't help it; there's a reason it's called the rock 'n' roll dream. And as Noel from Oasis said, "If you don't want to be a rock star, go fucking back to pumping gas." But these '90s bands, none of them could have anticipated how big they'd become: Pearl Jam sold over twenty-five million albums between 1991 and 1994 in the US alone. That's just crazy. We will never see songs as bleak as "Jeremy" or "Black Hole Sun" or "Vasoline" or "Man in the Box" reach that kind of audience ever again. The bands thought they were part of a counterculture, but I think what they didn't anticipate was that people were getting tired of music that was slick, calculated, and superficial. A lot of kids could relate to that deep layer of discontent.

I wasn't a kid in that era, I was playing those songs on the radio, but they were my soundtrack also; I was in a place where the music was speaking to me. I was going through a rough time in my marriage. I was a young father. I obviously had my own battles with drugs and alcohol. I was having some success, but there was a lot of disappointment and uncertainty. The guys in those bands were my generation, my peers, and they were expressing emotions that I was experiencing at that exact time. I can't even imagine going through the turmoil of that period without Soundgarden's *Badmotorfinger* and *Superunknown*, *Vs.*, Alice in Chains' *Dirt*, STP's *Core*. They were therapeutic for me. Part of my life was spinning out of control, and I personally needed that music so badly. I can't help thinking that there were millions of people going through the same thing.

The flip side of listeners using music as a valve to release the pressures, internal and external, that threaten to suffocate them is that too often there's no release for the people creating the music. As songwriters, musicians, singers, they're expected to burrow into their psyches, to go digging into dark areas, and what kind of toll does that take? Andrew, Kurt, Layne, Scott: from the moment we saw them we knew they were tapping into vast territories of pain, or else they were supernaturally gifted at acting as though they were. I don't know anyone who knew them who was shocked to hear the news of their deaths, but that didn't make those deaths any less devastating. It's the phone call, or text message, you dread: Layne's gone, or Scott. The music they made was stripped of glamour and pretending so millions of people could see themselves in it, but when it came to their own lives, they had nothing to cling to to get them through.

I was at the Reading Festival with Soundgarden for

Superunknown, hanging out in the rehearsal studio with Chris Cornell. He told me that when he was a kid, he was quite a loner. When his neighbors moved out, they left behind an entire Beatles record collection in their basement. Chris brought the records home, sat alone, and sang along. But what he said was, he would sing along and create a fourth voice. He wasn't singing John's, Paul's, or George's vocal line; he was doing an extra one, finding another harmony or melody line to sing, so he could add to it. His voice hadn't even broken yet. When he told me that story, I thought about my own experiences with records when I was a kid, my own little audio experiments alone in my basement. Chris and I made our own pathways. I think that's what we are: people who feel isolated, make a connection to the music, and, through that, a connection to others. In the end, we're a community of loners.

Encounters:
Oasis

With Liam Gallagher

I know that the way history is being written, their impact is considered less important than the arrival of Nirvana and the other Northwest bands, especially here in the States. But fuck that: I was crazy about them. That first album was a saving grace for me. I was at HTG when I heard the debut single "Supersonic," and the attitude and the snarl in that song floored me. It had more swagger than I'd heard in a song in a long time, and it reminded me in a way of all the British bands that I'd ever loved, from the Beatles and the Kinks to the Jam and the Clash. It was as though they synthesized all the best parts of what came before them, the melodic sense, the aggression, the ambition to take over the world.

Their album had this kind of lazy drumbeat that filled up with a thick, dense sound, and then Liam Gallagher's incredibly whiny voice. It was one of the most compelling things I'd heard in a while, since the start of the whole Nirvana–Soundgarden–Alice scene. I'd always kept up with the English scene—how could you grow up obsessed with rock and not?—but I didn't know what the future held for Oasis. The number of hot UK bands that were able to find success across the Atlantic was minimal. But I had a feeling about this one. I was friendly with a booking agent in Jersey, and he called me up: "Listen, do you think I should book this band Oasis? I got an offer, but I'm not sure." And I get it. There was only the one import single at that point, which I was playing on the air, but a lot of UK bands somehow got lost in translation on the way to America. The Wonder Stuff, Inspiral Carpets. I could go on and on . . .

"Do you think they'll sell any tickets?"

"Yeah, man. It'll sell out. It's the coolest thing I've heard lately."

"Really?"

"I'll tell you what: I'll make a deal with you. If it sells out, I want to introduce them, and I want you to pay me my old fee."

I'd made a decision based on a gut feeling from one single, but the gig was far enough away that I was thinking the buzz would grow. I hadn't heard "Live Forever" yet, or "Cigarettes and Alcohol," but I was such an optimist; if I hear a great song, I want that band to be fantastic. I want them to be larger than life. I believed these guys could be the British rock stars we'd been waiting for, the band we needed. I wanted to be a part of their story, to be the guy who got onstage and brought them on to play for an American crowd in South Jersey.

The show came up, the venue was at capacity, and I met these young guys from Manchester. Actually, it turned out that I'd met Noel Gallagher before: he had been to Jersey as a tech for Inspiral Carpets when they toured the States.

So Noel and Liam had these groupies with them who were looking to score some Charlie. I tracked down a local dealer friend of mine, another big music fan. He sold the band two eight-balls, which is like a quarter ounce of blow. Not only that, but the band made the girls pay for the drugs. That's rock 'n' roll: you buy us coke, we do it with you and fuck you later.

Another time when Oasis came through town, I was working at MTV, and Lewis Largent and I went to see them at Wetlands. He and I were the biggest Oasis fans at the station. Lewis was also a huge fan of the Rolling Stones. Liam went up to Lewis, got right in his face: "Stones or Beatles, man?" Lewis said Stones, and Liam goes, "Fuck you!" and tried to start a fistfight over it. Liam would come to blows over whether someone preferred the Stones to the Beatles, and Lewis wasn't one to take any shit, but he sure as hell wasn't going to brawl over what band is better. The thing about Oasis is, they really care about music to the point where they'd start a confrontation about it. Otherwise, what the fuck are you doing in a band?

The beauty of an Oasis song was that it was simple, and in its simplicity it was completely heartfelt and cut right to the center. Noel was, still is, one of the best songwriters to come out of England, and when you think about who else is on that list—Lennon and McCartney, Jagger and Richards, Ray Davies, Pete Townshend, later on Elton John and Elvis Costello, Kate Bush and Amy Winehouse—that's a really big statement. Noel once told me that when Nirvana released *Nevermind*, "That's when I knew with Oasis I could do the same kind of thing. I could turn up the distortion on my guitar but still sing pop melodies." He says that and I know he means it from the bottom of his heart. He makes no apologies, he doesn't try to hide anything. He says whatever the fuck he thinks, and that's why I love him so much. That's what it comes down to.

And it's not that I'm oblivious to the ways the band would stumble over their own feet, the infamous insanity, the behavior that some people might look at as self-sabotage. People cope with fame in different ways; some internalize their pain, some express it through their music, some just fuck up when it matters most. Oasis were masters of the wrong move, God bless them. MTV would put them up in a hotel and they'd order like every steak on the room service menu, then trash the suites. The talent person at the channel told me she almost lost her job. And then they were booked to do MTV *Unplugged*, which so many bands—including Nirvana—would tell you was maybe the biggest shot you could get at the station, a spotlight on a band that no other television appearance could match, and Liam decided that he didn't want to sing. Simple as that. Just not in the mood, too fucked up, or whatever. It had to go on without Liam. Though not completely. The whole time, he was sitting in the balcony looking down on the stage and heckling his brother and his band. That was how Liam was: he was hardly ever involved in any of the Oasis interviews I did throughout the years on MTV; once, he did show up, but spent the whole time looking out the window. I'd always talk to Noel or Bonehead, and everyone at Epic, including David Massey, who signed them for the US, knew that it was smarter to assume that Liam would flake.

I think about how big Oasis could have been in the United States if they had pulled their shit together. You can't explain something like that. Arrogance? Defiance? Just being out of your fucking skull? There were internal problems in the band, and a lack of willingness to tour; in their home country they were the biggest thing in years, and America was ripe for the taking, but that meant deciding to come over and not headline arenas right away. You've got to humble yourself a bit, and *humble* was not in the Gallagher dictionary (*cocaine* was, in bold type and underlined). And for me, unfortunately, their behavior was contagious. They were not a healthy influence, let's put it that way. I was asked to host a live broadcast in New York City in '95 when *(What's the Story) Morning Glory* came out, and before the show we drank a shitload of Jack Daniel's. The band handled it fine—it was standard preshow activity for them—but when I hit the mic, I was laughing and slurring my words, like a wino who'd stumbled into the studio. I remember that night as, "Oh, shit, I fucked this one up."

Now, in hindsight, Noel can look at an album like *Be Here Now* and be honest about the bombastic production fueled by shitloads of blow, the songs that went on and on. He sees how the material could have used some editing; that there was a pompous attitude behind it. He was one of those guys who, in the middle of it, lost perspective. Ultimately, to me, that's a tragedy in one way, but it doesn't change one bit the effect that Oasis had on me and my career.

"Live Forever" is such an important song to me, probably one of my favorite records ever, an amazing and beautiful song, filled with self-doubt, the realization that "You and I will never be all the things we want to be." But at the same time, it's hopeful. At that point, when it came out, I wasn't really sure where my life was heading. I was going through a divorce and wasn't living with my daughter Jessica. I had to pick her up and we'd drive around and listen to music. The Beatles, the Mamas and the Papas. We'd both sing along. It was a sad period in my life, and I'd lost one of my best friends, who also loved Oasis, to suicide. Along with all those '60s songs that we both loved, Jessica and I would sing "Live Forever."

Noel told me that when he heard Kurt Cobain's lyrics "I hate myself, I want to die," he thought, "How the fuck can you hate yourself and want to die? Fuck that. I want to live forever." Obviously, depression is complicated as fuck, and a lot of people don't understand that you can't just brush it away, that it isn't about not having the balls to buck up and face life head-on. But that inspired Noel to write "Live Forever." What I think is interesting is that Frances Bean, Kurt's daughter, said she was more of an Oasis girl than a Nirvana or grunge girl; that Oasis's songs make her cry.

M(att)TV

Matt rocking the crowd

One night I was at a show and ran into a promotion person from Atlantic Records. She introduced me to her boyfriend, Kurt Steffek, who was in the music department at MTV. Kurt was responsible for programming *120 Minutes*, the network's modern-rock show, for lack of a better description. I'd had a couple of drinks. I wasn't stupid slurring hammered, but you could tell. Steffek and I started talking, and I told him *120* was my favorite show on the channel. He said, "Man, I love your station. I live on Long Island near Amityville, and on my drive home I listen to you all the time. Look, we get hyped on everything, especially on *120*. Would you mind if I call you and track music with you? You're an alternative station, and I'd like to ask you what stuff you're getting a real temperature on, so when we have a decision to make I can say, 'Well, HTG says that people are really into this song,' or that no one gives a shit." So we became friendly, and he'd call me to get a read.

At the end of '92, I think it was, I read in one of the music trades that Dave Kendall wasn't going to be hosting *120* anymore. I immediately called Kurt.

"What happened with Kendall?"

"Well, you know, dude, they blew him out, and I don't know what they're going to do, but for now they're letting the artists host."

And I said, naïvely and arrogantly, but because I knew deep in my heart it was true, "You guys should hire someone like me to do the show, who the artists will respect, and who knows the music inside and out. Not someone who just reads what's on the prompter."

"I don't know if they'll think you're the demo."

Maybe they wanted someone young, or someone who wasn't bald.

He said he'd call me in a week. Instead he called in an hour and told me that Andy Schuon, the head of programming, wanted to bring me in for an audition. It didn't happen right away, and I guess they were thinking, "Well, we've got the bands doing it themselves right now, but what the hell, we'll try Matt out." My friend Steve Leeds, who went with me to the tryout, said I went wearing a Morrissey T-shirt that had a hole in it.

So I went to National, the old MTV studio, and there were maybe a dozen or more people in the room. They didn't give me any copy, just told me to start talking. They wanted me to riff. It was about a half hour of me telling about my radio thing, DJing in clubs, spinning alternative music, interviewing tons of artists. I thought it made total sense for me to be doing *120*, and I was excited about the prospect.

A little time went by, and I got a call saying Depeche Mode were coming up to MTV and they didn't want to host on their own. This was my shot. That's when the band had *Songs of Faith and Devotion* out, 1993. Dave Gahan was great, but Martin Gore was a little out of it and kind of looking the other way, making it really hard for me. I kept thinking, "This guy's going to fucking blow this for me. Oh, shit." But we got through taping the show, and I went back to Jersey, to the Melody, where I was still spinning. At midnight we stopped to watch me on *120*. When it was over, I thought it'd gone pretty well, but what mattered was what they thought at MTV.

I got a call from the head of on-air talent, Lauren Levine. She left me a voicemail message. "Matt, you were great on the air with Martin. I thought you were amazing and I want to talk to you more about it." So I was thinking, Shit, maybe I'll really get this. Then I was invited to meet with Andy, and later that day I had a session scheduled to interview Mike Scott from the Waterboys. I had a feeling something positive was happening. It turned out to be one of the biggest fucking buzzkills in my life.

"Matt," Andy said, "we thought you did a great job, but listen, Lewis Largent [an MTV exec] is going to do the show. We want to give him more of a profile here. But we want you to know you did a good job, and that we'll use you as a backup." I said thanks, and that I was grateful for the chance, but when I left the building my heart sunk to the bottom of my fucking stomach. Because at that point everyone in New Jersey—my friends, all the radio listeners that I had filled in about it—had seen or heard about the Depeche Mode show, and they were thinking I'd get the gig.

I had this feeling that something had died inside me, and I remember walking up the street to do the Waterboys thing, and how shitty I felt, and that I had to pull myself together. "Fuck, dude, you got another gig to do right now. Just fucking deal with this."

I knew I couldn't stay much longer at HTG. As cool as it was, I was making less money than a manager of a McDonald's, and for all its influence, the station was still low profile in a lot of ways. Industry friends like Tom Calderone and Steve Leeds kept telling me, "You need to be at a station that's registered with BDS"—an airplay monitoring service that tracks how records are doing in different markets—"if you want to matter. You've already taken HTG as far as you can." There was an opening at a rock station in Manchester, Vermont, that some MTV execs told me about.

I mean, I needed *something* to happen. It'd been like eleven years at the station, and thirteen at the Melody. And my marriage was in the shitter. On the rocks in a big way. It was a period where I was just like, "Fuck, am I going out in a blaze of glory soon? Am I going to be dead from all the drinking and drugging? Or am I going to pull my shit together and do other stuff?" I'd be in a car driving down the highway saying to myself, I better not get pulled over, because if I do, I'm going to slam into that fucking guardrail. When you use drugs and drink enough, you will get suicidal thoughts. You will get to the point where you're in a scary situation. I didn't want to kill myself, but I just didn't want the shame and the humiliation of the arrest.

I'll tell ya, my dog was named Lizzy, after Thin Lizzy, whose singer Phil Lynott died in his thirties. At one time, I had a cat named Keith Moon. I had named all my fucking animals after dead rock stars. I celebrated the life of chaos, and I thought that was living life to the fullest. Not realizing that it was so perilous. I'm not going to pretend I didn't have a shitload of fun, but drugs, they will take you out. There's only so much you can do to your heart.

Not to mention, New Brunswick was a death sentence for a lot of people. Literally. A lot of people who stayed around too long aren't around anymore. My best friend committed suicide, jumping from a dorm roof at Rutgers.

I knew I had to make a move, and at the same time I had to make enough money to help support my daughter. So I drove all the way up to this radio station in Vermont, WEQX. Their programmer, Jim McGuinn, was leaving. He'd broken the Spin Doctors' "Two Princes," picked the "No Rain" hit for Blind Melon, and done a hit edit for Rage Against the Machine's "Killing in the Name." I love him, and he's smart, and I consider him a kindred spirit. He was moving to St. Louis to run the Point, and recommended me to replace him. What went through my head the whole time was, I don't know where my life's going, but I should at least check it out.

The weekend was incredible. The first night, we went to the local bar next door to the station. It was funny, because it showed just how removed alternative music was. Even though it was still the most popular music in the country, the jukebox didn't have much of it. The bar was old Vermont, a hippie kind of vibe. We drank and played some classic songs on the jukebox, and I was put up in a ski lodge. Although I was happy to be there, I kept thinking how nice it would've been with someone, in a good relationship. Because here I go: my marriage is done, I'm at a career crossroads, I don't know what the fuck is going to happen.

I felt like I was going to take the job. I liked Brooks,

the station owner. He was a forward thinker, independent. We had a few more drinks on Sunday at Killington, and he said, "Why don't you do an on-air shift?" Right then, that afternoon. I could do a radio show even after a few cocktails. Brooks wanted to see if I could work on the fly.

After I did my impromptu shift, I got a call from a skier dude. He said, "Man, fuck, I listen to you every day on the radio. It was fucking crazy. We skied all day and drank all night, and I'm laying in the back of my friend's car and I hear your voice, and I'm like, 'Fuck, we're home already?' " He had another six or so hours to drive. He thought he was home. He thought he'd made it back to New Jersey.

When I made it back, Brooks called me. We had never talked money. He made me an offer.

"I love your place and I want to do it, but Brooks, I gotta make more money than that. How am I going to see my daughter and bring her up here?"

"No, listen, man. We can promote those concerts like me and Jim did with the Spin Doctors and Blind Melon."

There was no guarantee that was going to happen, because there was competition from local promoters and from another rock station. I couldn't do it. I told him no, and hung up. I think he changed his mind and tried to call me back, but I had a bad gut feeling about it. Not about the station. Just, if I'm going to fight over money now, that little money, how the fuck am I going to survive later on? Something told me not to pick up the phone. No disrespect to Brooks. It didn't feel right. We weren't even in the right neighborhood.

Two things happened after that: Patti Galluzzi from MTV told me they were looking for a new program director at WBRU up in Rhode Island, and a few days later, I got a call from Andy Schuon, also at MTV.

"Matt, three of the people in our music department are leaving. I'd love for you to come up."

Who says there are no second chances?

I met with Andy, and that went really well. I told Patti, "I know you were talking to me about my going to BRU and moving to Providence, but I'd rather keep living in Jersey and be at MTV." Obviously, BRU is a great station, but MTV at that point was the biggest rock station in America.

Andy said he'd give me a call later on.

I went back to Asbury Park to do my air shift. And I was worried that Andy was going to call me back and the line would be busy. HTG was still a mom-and-pop radio station. It only had four phone lines: 800, 881, 882, 883. If the sales department and the front office were on the phone, the lines were tied up. You couldn't get through. What if Andy tried to offer me the job but couldn't get through? What if that gave him time to change his mind? 'Cause, I mean, you never know.

"Matt, Andy Schuon is on the phone for you."

I found an empty room. There weren't many in the house.

Andy said, "Hey, I'm sorry. The phone was busy, and I've been trying to call you for like two hours."

"Yeah, there're only four lines here and . . ."

"Matt, I'll tell you what. Come work for me, and I'll make sure you have more than four lines in your office."

And that was the phone call that changed my life.

Buzz Clips and Twists of Fate

My leaving HTG for MTV was kind of a big deal, in New Jersey at least. There was a story on it in the *Asbury Park Press*. I had mixed feelings about leaving, and when it came time to do my final show, I honestly didn't know if that was the end of my career in radio. So I stayed on the air for eight hours, playing all the records I loved. Well, not all the records I loved; that would have taken much longer than an eight-hour shift. The DJ who was supposed to go on after my normal shift told me to stay on as long as I wanted. I knew moving on was the smart thing to do. I wanted the opportunity to help influence pop culture on a national scale, and I needed to push my career forward to take care of my daughter. For all the power HTG had, far beyond what anyone could ever have predicted, it wasn't paying a hell of a lot of money. I had to take this shot.

I started at MTV at a moment when they were scrambling to reposition themselves. Around that time, they announced that they were canceling *Headbangers Ball*, a flagship show for all things hard rock. They were responding to what was happening in the market; you couldn't ignore that bands like Pearl Jam were selling a million albums in just one week.

They and other "grunge" bands were redefining the louder side of rock. *Headbangers* had a connotation that was no longer cool. That's too bad. You can make fun of the clichés of heavy metal all you like, stereotype it in terms of its excesses, the over-the-top posturing, the idea of the metal kids being, let's say, less nuanced and discriminating in their musical tastes. But a lot of people grew up on it and had a lot of affection for it, the way I'd loved music like KISS, Slade, and T. Rex when I was younger. I could relate, and I was at heart still a hard rock kid.

Because I was associated, on the radio, with the alternative side of the spectrum and had shown foresight in identifying what bands were ultimately going to matter, it made sense from MTV's perspective to get me on board. It was the craziest time to get there. Look at any chart of the biggest rock songs of 1994 and you'll get the idea: this bulldozer had roared onto the rock landscape, leveled the whole infrastructure, and built up this new community where "Interstate Love Song," "Better Man," "All Apologies," "Black Hole Sun," "No Excuses," "Vasoline," "Basket Case," and "Come Out and Play" dominated the year-end charts. Hell, "Backwater" by the Meat Puppets was a big airplay song. The fucking Meat Puppets. At the start of the '90s, all of this would have been completely unthinkable. And there was a stampede by the major labels to get a piece of the New Thing, even if many of the entrenched record executives couldn't make sense of it. They were just chasing a notion of "alternative." It was completely insane: Chrysalis Records, not a major, but surely a respected label with a distinguished track record going back to the '60s, would sign a band called Butt Trumpet, whose album was titled *Primitive Enema*. Some songs on that album: "Classic Asshole," "Ode to Dickhead," "Clusterfuck." "Clusterfuck," come to think of it, isn't a bad description of the hordes of A&R people being dispatched to the Northwest to snap up any band that was still left unsigned after "Smells Like Teen Spirit" started the gold rush.

My title was Manager of Music Programming and Talent. At the station, we'd sit in meetings every week like the music industry's tribunal, determining what clips we'd add and in what rotation, what had to be dropped, what videos went into specialty programming, which went to the reject pile. It was an insane amount of power in the hands of maybe ten people, and the pressure from within the record business reflected how much was at stake. The lobbying was intense; reps from the labels told us that their jobs were on the line if we didn't add a specific video, or if it wasn't put in the Buzz Bin, or if we decided after a few spins that a video wasn't working for us. They'd come with reams of research, airplay statistics, tour grosses, anything to convince us that this artist should be a priority for MTV. There was considerable arm-twisting going on at the very highest corporate level, record company presidents calling MTV executives and using every coercive tactic they could think of, because so much was at stake. In 1995, MTV was still a gigantic cultural influence, with the power to break bands or cast them into a pile of musical rubble. So these meetings were taken very seriously and watched very closely. We'd meet in the conference room, and we'd watch maybe thirty-five videos every week. Most of them, we sat through the whole thing, unless it was absolutely terrible. The acquisition meetings lasted two and a half, three hours, and we had lists of all the videos we were considering adding. We tried not to let the industry agendas get in the way.

We knew which bands mattered to the labels, but that didn't mean they mattered to us, although sometimes we'd throw something into light rotation to give it a shot. We'd sit there with our Xeroxed lists and mark what was going to happen with those videos. We made a lot of record executives apoplectic. They'd come back a second or third time with the same clip but some new information, some sales story, some regional activity, some big radio station ad. Or they'd invite us all out for drinks and dinner, or concerts. Ninety percent of the time we went out as a gang, and we absolutely had the sense that we were sitting in the circle of power. But I was humble enough, I think, to realize that I was learning the ropes about that side of the music business, in terms of mechanics and politics. I'd done programming at HTG, so I was well aware of the promotion game, but this was a whole new sphere. My mission, as I saw it, was to make sure the bands who deserved a shot got one.

Looking back, everything feels inevitable, everything falls into place. You see the careers of the giant bands, U2, Coldplay, Oasis, Radiohead, and you can't imagine that anything could have happened any differently than it did, like there was an alignment in the universe that made it all possible. But what you find out, when you're on the inside, is that there is a very thin line between the bands who survive and the ones who get left by the side of the road. It's so precarious, so unpredictable. It could all turn on the passion of one or two key individuals. Radiohead could have easily been an act remembered for "Creep" and nothing else. It almost happened: Radiohead's next album, *The Bends*, came out, and a lot of people on the radio side decided there wasn't a single. They barely gave the band a shot. They're a perfect example of how gatekeepers can almost be a career-blocking obstacle, and how people sitting in another room can right the course of musical history. I don't think people remember how on the edge Radiohead were, what a factor MTV was in keeping their momentum alive.

One of the reasons MTV brought me in to begin with was that they'd already been running music past me and they knew I wouldn't bullshit them. I had so much respect for what they were doing, and I'd hoped to have a future with them. I wasn't sure that would ever happen, but I was in the mix, telling them the truth about what I thought about certain records and certain bands. So when I got into the MTV war room, I knew that these ten or so people literally had the ability to change a band's complete future. That was how much influence MTV still had at that point. Blind Melon was just one example. I mean, maybe Capitol signed the band because Shannon Hoon had done vocals on a Guns N' Roses track, and that's how record companies are: if you're associated with a superstar, they'll give you a shot, thinking maybe some of that mojo will rub off. Capitol put out "Tones of Home" as the first single, but when "No Rain" emerged as the real hit, and MTV put its Buzz Bin stamp on it, that was the game changer for the band. It happened over and over: White Zombie were doing okay, and then Mike Judge used one of their tracks on *Beavis and Butthead* and it exploded. MTV saw what was going on when the Dave Matthews Band began building a college following, and after they got signed to RCA, the station helped break them nationally. They were paying attention.

I'd heard the story about how at MTV, long before I got there, back in '87, there was a lot of resistance to adding Guns N' Roses. But one MTV VP, Sheri Howell, fought for "Welcome to the Jungle." She was adamant. Whether she was getting flak from Geffen Records about it, I don't know, but she wouldn't shut up about this band and this video. One night at a restaurant she was with her MTV colleagues and went on her Guns rant, and someone finally said, "Sheri, if you get up and dance on the table, we'll add the video." And no one thought she'd do it, because she was pretty shy and sensitive, but she got up on the table and danced. She was willing to stand up and testify for the band, and you have to admire that. I always wanted to be the person loud enough and determined enough to stand on the table, even though no one would offer me anything to start dancing.

All big rock success stories seem preordained. But so often it takes a person literally getting up on the table to make people listen. You look at Guns N' Roses and think, Axl and Slash, and those songs, the punk attitude, the metal roots. People get on autopilot and think they have a formula figured out, and then something comes along that rips up the playbook the way Guns did, just by being a synthesis of all the different music they loved.

The whole music department, including me and Lewis Largent, were super passionate about Radiohead, despite the prevailing opinion that *The Bends* lacked a "Creep"-y track. With every video that came in—"Fake Plastic Trees," "High and Dry," "Street Spirit (Fade Out)"—we flipped out. "Just" is one of my favorite videos of the decade. It's really a striking piece of film: there's a guy lying on the sidewalk, and people keep walking up to him asking him why he's there. It reminded me of a *Twilight Zone* episode in a way; you're hearing the song, and the band is playing in the building across the street. Everything is in subtitles. The guy says if he told you why he's lying in the street, you wouldn't be able to handle it. At that time, people weren't afraid of making really avant-garde, artistic videos. The people are screaming, and then there are no titles, you don't know what he's saying, and the camera pulls back and everyone's lying on the ground next to the guy. It just blew me away.

We took so much shit from every other record label for playing "Just" so heavily. They would come in with their sales figures and show us how their record was outselling Radiohead—which wasn't that much, truthfully, but it didn't matter. People would come in and argue with us, scream at us, because they wanted that slot. We were standing behind something that we thought was special. We did not budge from that record.

I'd been a fan of theirs from the beginning, and we met for the first time when *Pablo Honey* was out and they were playing New York City. They had a night off, and they asked Christine Biller, who worked for Ignition, Radiohead's UK management firm, what they should do on a Sunday night in Manhattan. And she said, Fuck going to clubs in the city. You've got to drive down to New Brunswick, New Jersey, and go listen to Matt Pinfield spin records. So Radiohead got in a white van, drove down, and hung out with me all night. I took them out for their first experience at a Jersey diner.

Finally, *The Bends* went gold, and the band and people from Capitol came up to MTV to give us plaques for that.

I believe we were certainly one of the major factors. The press caught up with us; they started to think maybe they missed something with this album, didn't give it proper attention. At this little presentation, Thom Yorke came up to me, Andy Schuon, and Lewis Largent—the three of us had been chatting in the corner—and he said, "You know, I realize you took a lot of shit to back up this record, and I just want to tell you how much it means to me, and how much we appreciate it . . ." and he broke into tears and walked away. It was such a pinnacle moment in his career, that this album broke through for his band, and then of course *OK Computer* came out in '97. But things could have so easily taken a wrong turn if *The Bends* had faded away without us giving it a shot. People don't realize how much hangs in the balance for bands, how quickly it can all go away, that support from one source can make such a difference.

You have to have conviction and be able to express it. I believed in the band 311, and based on the airplay we'd given them at HTG while I was still there, I watched them build their audience from basically nothing. They were booked to play the Fast Lane in Jersey and were paid like $200 and a pizza, and they sold the fucking place out. So when their self-titled album came out in '95 and I was in the MTV conference room, I fought for them. I was comparing them, and I know it's kind of a stretch, to what had happened with Green Day, how the indie following had built and spread, and I told the other people in the room that they needed to pay attention. One guy in the music department looked at me and said, "Matt, you must be on drugs," and I said, "I'm actually not, today." Then Andy Schuon said, "You know, just because of Matt's passion"—and I'm sure that's true, because there was no real love for the band anywhere else in that meeting—"we're going to make this a Buzz Clip." Well, that turned out to be the band's breakthrough, with "Down," "Don't Stay Home," and "All Mixed Up." The album sold over three million copies, and you have to give MTV credit for that, at least for getting it started and being committed to making it happen.

After they decided to give 120 to Lewis Largent, I thought that spelled the end of my on-air television career. The Depeche Mode Incident had gone just okay, but I had to accept the fact that maybe I had, as the saying goes, "a face made for radio." Imagine all the teenage girls in their basements watching MTV late at night and I come on their screen, this bald barrel of a person with a voice like granite, spouting arcane rock trivia. If you're a TV executive, you might want to spare America. But in '95, Lewis said, "Why the fuck am I hosting this? I like being Vice President of Programming. Matt should be hosting 120." He had decided that he wanted to be behind the scenes and let someone else do the show, but the execs, for all the reasons cited above, were not about to turn the show over to me. Instead they let the artists do it themselves. Fine. Until the guys in Oasis decided that they didn't want to host, and MTV needed someone on camera to interview the band. They decided to give me a three-week period to do the show and see if I could make it work, starting with the Oasis episode.

I was ready to do it: I knew the studio so well, I knew the band, I was confident that I had the musical knowledge. But I hadn't been in front of a camera before except for that Depeche Mode audition, so I was a little stiff, and afraid that, once again, I wouldn't end up getting the job. I liked my job behind the scenes, and I told myself that it wouldn't be the worst thing in the world if I got passed over. One part of my brain was convinced that I'd never be on radio or TV again. That's how I psyched myself up to do the Oasis interview for *120: no agenda*. I decided to relax and wing it. I started a skirmish on the set between Bonehead and Noel about their favorite football teams, Manchester City or United, and while they were battling it out, I looked at the camera and said, "While these guys are fighting, we're going to break for a commercial . . ." It was good television. Bonehead tried to wind me up, making a crack about Paul Weller, and I reached over and smacked him in the head. That was cool as fuck.

Right after the show was taped, Lauren Levine, the head of talent for MTV, came up to me and said—I'll never forget this—"I am doing a complete one-eighty. You should be doing the show every fucking week." The twenty-one-day probation period was lifted. I had the gig as the permanent host of *120 Minutes*, a show that for nearly a decade had come to represent the most progressive, outside-the-box programming on the channel. It's not like I didn't think I deserved the gig, because I certainly knew I did, but there are all kinds of factors I had no control over. They could have said, We need somebody younger, or a woman, or someone British, or someone with a head of hair, or a team of identical Irish twins, or a rock star. You never know. I was prepared to be told, *Thanks, but we're going in a different direction.* Instead, I was given this platform to expose music that I loved and interview artists on the air. That gave me so much credibility and visibility, and I became one of the most recognizable people on the station. They used me in all types of situations: in one contest they superimposed my head into a bunch of old videos, like Madonna's "Vogue." They spent an entire weekend playing the Top 500 Videos of

All Time, and if viewers spotted me, they had the chance to win $50,000. They put me in a show called *Celebrity Death Match*, on an episode called "The Battle of the Non-Network Stars," and had me fighting, and beating, Jesse Camp. (Remember him? He was the winner of the Wanna Be a VJ contest in 1998.)

I guess you can safely say you've arrived when, like Bruce Springsteen, Tom Cruise, and other iconic cultural figures, you're parodied by Ben Stiller. It was a shock to me to see Stiller, at the 1998 MTV Music Awards, wearing a bald cap, an oversize shirt, and, I assume, considerable midsection padding and imitating my bear-awoken-from-hibernation voice. He spouted arcane musical references: "If you trace the entire history of rock music from the Weavers up to the 13th Floor Elevators, take a pit stop at Kansas, you'll eventually end up at Beck." He confronted Beck for an interview, and Beck looked at him incredulously and walked away. It cracked me up, because he captured me so well, and it was such an honor to be lampooned by him, especially during his breakthrough year when *There's Something about Mary* became a box-office smash. It was surreal, and I thought for a second, "Is this an insult? Or a compliment?" And then I thought, This movie star dressed up like me for three and a half hours, and even if he's making complete fun of me, all my mannerisms and quirks, it says that I'm a part of pop culture. It means I'm identifiable and recognizable, that people will get the joke. It's like being parodied on *Saturday Night Live*. I decided to accept it as an honor that will live forever courtesy of YouTube.

When *120* started in the '80s, it was a late-night outpost

for niche music, but in the second half of the '90s, during my tenure there, what did that even mean? I knew I had to preserve what was special about the premise of *120 Minutes* while attracting the younger brothers and sisters of the original *120* viewers. Things were different, sure, and influences were changing, but that's how it always is; there's a fluid generational migration that goes on constantly. The next group of kids has to find its own meaning, and that's who I was doing *120* for. Almost every day I have someone come up to me and say, "I learned everything about music from you. You and MTV and *120* were my only source where I grew up." Because as much as radio mattered, there were so many places throughout the US—not to mention around the world—where there was no radio outlet for alternative music. If you lived in New York, Chicago, or Los Angeles, any big city, you were tapped into whatever was hot, but in wide stretches of the US there was nothing but the sound of crickets and country music, maybe a Top 40 station or easy listening. And if you were a kid in middle school somewhere in, I don't know, Iowa or Wyoming or South Dakota, and you were desperate to hear rock music that gets into your bloodstream, there was nowhere to turn. There are no rock clubs for hundreds of miles, and maybe you're fourteen or fifteen and don't even have a driver's license. There's no K-Rock. What there was was MTV, and I saw *120* as this secret place where those kids could feel a part of something bigger.

As I said, I thought MTV could have kept the *Headbangers Ball* brand and tweaked it to acknowledge the new reality, but after I was doing *120* for a little while, the station decided to also give me a daily show called *Matt Rock*. It was essentially a revamped *Headbangers*, where I could play Ozzy, Metallica, new-generation metal bands like Korn and Limp Bizkit. Jimmy Page and Robert Plant came by the show; so did Van Halen, Rob Zombie, and Dave and Taylor from Foo Fighters. It was a place for Pantera, and the Rollins Band. It's weird: people are always putting up musical barricades, but doing 120 and *MattRock* and getting feedback, you know that a lot of that division is arbitrary and artificial. You can't typecast anyone. I was backstage once with Rob Zombie, a quintessential metal guy, and he was playing Jim Croce songs. Philip Anselmo, the lead singer from Pantera, said in an interview that his favorite bands growing up were the Cure and the Smiths.

I'm very, very fortunate that I was given the freedom to support things out of true love and not worry about category. If I liked a band, it didn't matter what people thought or where they wanted to slot them. 120 and *MattRock* may have been geared toward separate audiences, but I know there was plenty of overlap. People could see the complete spectrum of the music that meant the most to me. Sometimes I had to fight to get artists on my shows; there were people at MTV who didn't want me to put on the Descendents or Superchunk. There was a little battle, for some reason, over Duncan Sheik. I didn't care; I thought Duncan was an exceptional songwriter, and when I heard "Barely Breathing" from his debut album, it didn't matter whether he "fit" or not. Ten years later, his *Spring Awakening* was on Broadway.

Is Marilyn Manson metal? Alternative? Does it matter? He's a provocative artist, and he was responsible for provoking one MTV viewer to threaten to kill me for having him on my show. He was "one of God's soldiers," this character, and to him I was in cahoots with the devil for associating myself with Marilyn Manson. He left messages on my office phone, and MTV had to have security guards take me out of the building. I did feel that my life was in danger. Manson caused trouble. Once, when I was going through a rough time, I decided to go to my friend José's house down the shore. The phone rang, and José answered it.

"I want to do a line of coke off your cock."

"Who *is* this?"

"Is this Matt?"

Manson was calling to see if I wanted to hang out with him and Twiggy (his guitarist, not the slender UK super-model, alas), but José did look at me very strangely when he handed me the phone. "Matt, it's for you." For the record, not that I'm being judgmental about anyone's private behavior, no one has ever snorted a line of coke off my cock.

MTV changed the entire game for me; I was meeting and interviewing my heroes, working with people that I loved, picking people's brains, making what I think was a real impact on the culture. There's footage of me singing an a cappella "Sweet Emotion" with Steven Tyler. MTV gave me an online show, *Take It to the Matt*, where anybody who was on the internet then—not that many people, but it was building—would throw rock trivia questions at me, and that turned into *Stump Matt* on the TV network. It was a blast, the whole MTV experience. It was my home base until 1999, when, as it had to so many people, the lure of California beckoned, the land of Brian Wilson and Jim Morrison. Hollywood! Movie stars!

50 ESSENTIAL ROCK ALBUMS:
THE '90s

The Afghan Whigs—*Gentlemen*

Alice in Chains—*Dirt*

Bad Religion—*Stranger than Fiction*

Beastie Boys—*Check Your Head*

Beck—*Odelay*

Blur—*Parklife*

Jeff Buckley—*Grace*

Cypress Hill

Depeche Mode—*Violator*

Dr. Dre—*The Chronic*

Foo Fighters—*There Is Nothing Left to Lose*

Garbage

Green Day—*Dookie*

Happy Mondays—*Pills 'n' Thrills and Bellyaches*

Hole—*Live Through This*

Jane's Addiction—*Ritual de lo Habitual*

Kid Rock—*Devil Without a Cause*

Korn—*Life Is Peachy*

Lenny Kravitz—*Mama Said*

The La's

Live—*Throwing Copper*

Marilyn Manson—*Antichrist Superstar*

Metallica (The Black Album)

Morrissey—*Your Arsenal*

Neutral Milk Hotel—*In the Aeroplane over the Sea*

Nine Inch Nails—*The Downward Spiral*

Nirvana—*Nevermind*

Oasis—*(What's the Story) Morning Glory?*

Pantera—*Vulgar Display of Power*

Pavement—*Crooked Rain, Crooked Rain*

Pearl Jam—*Vs.*

PJ Harvey—*Rid of Me*

Primal Scream—*Screamadelica*

The Prodigy—*Fat of the Land*

Radiohead—*The Bends*

Rage Against the Machine

Rancid—*. . . And Out Come the Wolves*

Red Hot Chili Peppers—*Blood Sugar Sex Magik*

R.E.M.—*Automatic for the People*

The Smashing Pumpkins—*Siamese Dream*

Soundgarden—*Superunknown*

Stone Temple Pilots—*Purple*

Teenage Fanclub—*Bandwagonesque*

Temple of the Dog

Tool—*Ænima*

Urge Overkill—*Saturation*

U2—*Achtung Baby*

The Verve—*Urban Hymns*

Weezer (The Blue Album)

The Wonder Stuff—*Never Loved Elvis*

Jimmy and Doug's Farm:
LA and the Dawn of the Digital Age

Jimmy Iovine and N.W.A

I didn't imagine that I'd end up in California, even though I'd gone there a lot all during the '90s for one professional reason or another. Once I flew out there for an opportunity to become a movie star. Or at least to act opposite one. I got an incredible letter from the director-writer Cameron Crowe, who (almost) famously got his start as a rock journalist for *Rolling Stone*. Out of nowhere, I was contacted by a casting agent telling me there was a potential part for me in the next Crowe film, *Jerry Maguire*. At first I thought someone was fucking with me: there was no way Cameron Crowe even knew who I was, let alone thought I could be in a movie, but I asked my pal Rick Krim, a friend of Cameron's, and sure enough, it was for real. This was a huge deal: Crowe had written *Fast Times at Ridgemont High*, and his previous film *Singles* showed a keen grasp of modern rock culture, even casting Eddie Vedder as one of the members of Matt Dillon's fictional Seattle band Citizen Dick. Crowe knew his stuff.

"There are only two people who don't have to audition for this film, Tom Cruise and Matt Pinfield," Cameron said when we got in touch. He was going to put me in this scene where I was a news guy yelling at Cruise at the Marriott Marquis. Crowe was going to coach and direct me. We talked about it back and forth, and I was trying to balance my MTV schedule. I shot some footage of me "acting" in an empty MTV studio from a script he sent me so he could have something on tape. There were a couple of scenes he was thinking of using me in. One wound up going to Jerry Cantrell from Alice in Chains, who played a Kinko's guy, but Crowe had another one in mind, an interviewer at the football draft in Phoenix where Cruise goes with Cuba Gooding Jr.

I was going to fly out. This was going to be my dream. Then Cameron told me they had to cut that scene from the script because they went overbudget shooting a football scene. There went my big movie break.

Maybe a year later, I was in LA to host 120 from the K-Rock Almost Acoustic Christmas at the Universal Amphitheatre. I got a call from Cameron. "Listen, Matt, I'm sorry I couldn't put you in the film, but why don't you come hang out with us while we edit?" On Saturday, I ran over to Sony Studios in Culver City and watched Cameron edit a scene from *Jerry Maguire*. I remember that there was a movie poster on the wall for the upcoming film *One Fine Day*, with George Clooney and Michelle Pfeiffer, and Cameron and his music supervisor, Danny Bramson, saying, "I think our biggest competition is going to be that Clooney–Pfeiffer movie. We gotta worry about that." Cameron told me that Cruise would do every single interview, do anything he could to promote *Jerry Maguire*. Ultimately, they didn't have to worry about *One Fine Day* stealing the attention, the reviews, or the box office. *Jerry Maguire* was a breakthrough for Crowe, nominated for Best Film and Best Actor at the Oscars, and I still think if I'd been a little luckier it might've been me instead of Cuba Gooding Jr. accepting that Best Supporting Actor award. Okay, maybe not.

The next day, after the visit with Cameron and Danny at Sony, there was a barbecue at Jessica Entner's house. Jessica was the daughter of Warren Entner, the manager of Rage Against the Machine, Faith No More, and other bands. Warren had so many great stories from the '60s, when he was a member of the hit group the Grass Roots. Jessica was also, at the time, Carson Daly's girlfriend. Carson was hosting a night show on K-Rock, and we had just met a few days earlier. So we were all hanging out at her place—me, Carson, and a guy from Mojo Records that had some hip ska bands like Goldfinger and Reel Big Fish. It was a lovely LA day, and I remember Carson mentioned that he really wanted to make the jump from radio to television. I suppose since he knew that I'd made the transition, he thought I might have some career advice. I gave him the name of an MTV talent guy and said, "Give him a call. MTV is going to be doing *Hotel California*, a summerhouse show in LA, and you'd be perfect for it." He got the gig and of course wound up being the host of MTV's *Total Request Live*, and it all started on that couch at that LA party.

I found out on my trips to LA that clichés are clichés because they're fucking true. Like everyone else on this planet, I'd always heard stories about what went on at the Playboy

Mansion but didn't have the chance to see for myself until I got invited there to celebrate the 1999 song of the year, Limp Bizkit's "Nookie." I'm not sure that was the song of the year for everybody, but for the purpose of a party at Hefner's house, "Nookie" was a no-brainer. You had to wear pajamas at this soiree, and I was coming from a different shoot, so I had to change into my pj's in the car on the way over, not a pretty sight. We got to the mansion, and it's everything you picture a party there would be. It's probably the only place on the planet where half-naked young women "frolic." You'd think "frolicking" was an outdated notion, but not in Hef World. I walked past Bill Maher, hammered and stumbling across the lawn. Ben Stiller and his wife were there. I hung out at one of the bars for a while talking about music with Leonardo DiCaprio, and all of a sudden I realized that I desperately needed to pee. So I walked over to the primary bathroom near the lair (like *frolic*, *lair* is a word that is only appropriate to use if you're on the actual grounds of this property).

There was a long line of people in their pajamas waiting to use the bathroom, so I decided to try to find another bathroom somewhere else. Someone pointed me to the game room. I followed the general direction—I'd had a few drinks myself and might have been slightly impaired—and I opened what I thought was the bathroom. Oops. It was a bedroom, and what I saw were two drummers from separate platinum rock bands (I didn't know drummers had such an intimate bond) having sex simultaneously with two Playboy Bunnies. The guys were entangled with these accommodating young women, and one of the drummers looked up, basically did a one-handed push-up (drummer upper-body strength is quite impressive), and waved at me: "Hi, Matt!"

Like he was actually happy to see me. Under similar circumstances, I don't think I'd have been as friendly.

"Hey, guys. Sorry I barged in on you. I was just looking for the bathroom."

"Oh, it's right around the corner over there."

I took a piss, then passed by the room on the way back. They were still engaged in this naked foursome, but one of the drummers, a very polite guy, waved to me. "Bye, Matt! Take care!" That was my Playboy Mansion encounter, and to tell the truth, I'd have been disappointed if it had gone any differently. If you're going to a party at Hef's, you want to stroll around in pajamas, see naked boobs in the grotto, knock back some drinks with DiCaprio, and walk in on a couple of rock drummers going down on two Bunnies.

I was zipping back and forth between New York and LA a lot. I had the *MattRock* show on MTV, and that was East Coast–based, but so many of the hard rock bands were still out west. On assignment for a Van Halen piece, I got out there right around the time when there were all these mudslides. So it was a muddy ride out to Eddie Van Halen's studio 5150, out toward Malibu in the hills. Alex and I met up outside 5150 and talked for around forty-five minutes. Then I went inside, and when I went to use the bathroom, I saw a quarter-inch jack for a guitar in the wall underneath the roll of toilet paper. I asked Eddie what that was all about, and he said that sometimes he brings his guitar into the bathroom when he's taking a dump and tries out riffs. The jack connected to the studio. Genius.

Eddie's an obsessive musician. He told me, when we were in the studio, that he'd sent back the new album to the mastering studio around twenty-three times trying to get it right. That's one thing anyone making music can tell you:

you can work on something infinitely. It's never "finished." It reaches a point where you slump in your chair and say "enough." Because you can always tweak it some more, add or subtract something, raise or lower a vocal, change a guitar riff. I know a lot of musicians who can't let go; someone from the record company has to come and almost physically rip the tape out of their hands. From what I've seen, Eddie is like that. That night, after everyone else in the studio had left for dinner, he and I stuck around and he played me some tracks from the new album, until finally we left to grab a bite at a Thai place nearby.

I invited my *MattRock* producer Austin Redding to join us for dinner. He was a total rocker, and had a Van Halen tattoo on his arm that he was kind of embarrassed to show Eddie. "Come on, Austin," I teased him. "Roll up your sleeve." Austin was a medic in the first Iraq War, the Bush Sr. one, saved a lot of lives, and survived that shit and came back to get a gig producing TV. That night at the Thai place, we all started talking about our relationships, and Austin said that he wanted to ask his girlfriend to marry him. I said, "Wouldn't it be fucking cool to get engaged onstage with Van Halen?" Kidding around, but the band said they were into it. I didn't think anything of it after that. But sure enough, they got in touch with me when they were coming to New York to play the Garden and wanted to go ahead with it. I was shooting a *Beach House* show for MTV down in Seaside Heights, on the Jersey Shore, and naturally we hit all kinds of summer traffic driving back into the city, and I was in the car thinking, Oh, God, I can't believe I'm going to blow this opportunity. We got there late and missed the opening act, a new band called Creed.

Austin's girlfriend thought she was coming to the show

to see me sing backup on "Jump" during the band's encore. I walked out onstage after the main set, and the crowd started screaming, maybe because they were happy to see me, maybe because it meant Van Halen was going to do another song, who knows? There was so much energy. It's fucking Madison Square Garden!

"Hey, everybody," I started in. "One of my best friends, and the producer of my show *MattRock*, his dream has always been to be onstage with Van Halen at the Garden, so we're going to make that happen tonight, so I hope you'll clap for him." The place went berserk. I handed Austin the microphone. "Matt's right; it has always been my dream to be onstage with Van Halen, but I've got something much more important to do right now." Eddie Van Halen and Michael Anthony took Austin's girlfriend's arms and walked her out to the center of the stage, and Austin dropped to his knees, took out a ring, and asked her to marry him. It's all being shown on the big arena screen. Eddie, Michael, and I are standing there, and she says yes, and then the band played "Jump." The fact that I was able to give that moment to Austin, that meant so much, and I was at their wedding. I got pretty wild that night and did one of the bridesmaids. It worked out well for everyone.

It was Austin, who was running his own production company in LA, who gave me my next big job tip. "Hey, I hear Doug Morris and Jimmy Iovine are looking for a host for a TV show. You should check it out." Everything is connected. I knew who Morris and Iovine were; everybody in the music business did. Doug started out in the industry writing songs for Laurie Records acts like the Chiffons and the Barbarians (including their classic "Are You a Boy or Are You a Girl?"), and even had a fleeting recording career of his own ("I'm Gonna Be with You" on ABC-Paramount, "Frigid Digit" on Epic) before becoming one of the most successful record executives at Atlantic, Warners, Universal, and Sony. Iovine began as an engineer and producer (Tom Petty and the Heartbreakers, Stevie Nicks, U2) before forming Interscope Records in 1990. (Today, Morris runs all of Sony Music and Iovine has a senior position at Apple.) Back in '99, Morris and Iovine were the hottest team: everything they touched at Universal and Interscope was blowing up, and whatever they had in mind for this TV show, I knew that it was something I had to check out. Besides, being at MTV at the end of the decade meant having my rock outpost relegated to something of an afterthought. The biggest things on the station were Britney Spears's ". . . Baby One More Time" and Backstreet Boys' "I Want It That Way"; NSYNC, Ricky Martin, and Christina Aguilera were all selling millions of albums; and the only rock album to wind up on the year-end list of top albums was Kid Rock's *Devil Without a Cause*. I'm a big pop fan and always have been, but in the world of MTV, most of the action was over at *TRL*. It only made practical sense for me to put out feelers, and Andy Schuon, who had been such a strong advocate of mine at MTV, was now out in LA and was going to be a part of Doug and Jimmy's new venture.

It wasn't so much that I had my mind set on LA. I had a brand-new place in Clifton, New Jersey, a three-bedroom apartment with a wide balcony, not too expensive. I liked where I was, geographically, at least. But I wasn't sure there was a future at MTV for what I wanted to do; I didn't want to be the rock guy in a pop world, holding down the fort after the battle had already been lost. Around the same time, there was a chance I might be hired for an A&R job at Epic

Records. I had become friendly with David Massey during the early Oasis period, and we stayed in touch. He knew how deeply into music I was, and we talked about another band he'd signed, Silverchair, and he said he'd run the idea around the label of my joining the A&R staff. He had to work the room on my behalf. He set up a dinner with him, me, and Epic's president, Polly Anthony, and it seemed obvious that she was looking for someone who might bring in more instant-pop artists. She was quizzing me, like about which act out there would I have wanted to sign, and I probably said someone like Foo Fighters when I think she was hoping I would say something more along the lines of Backstreet Boys. That was the climate at the time. I got it. They wanted to compete in boy-band nation, or find someone to be Epic's Britney or Christina. (That summer, not that long after our meeting, Epic released the first single by Mandy Moore, "Candy.") That's how it works at record companies. By the way, I have no problem with the whole pop/boy-band phenomenon. Tween girls have been right more often than not; they were right to squeal for Sinatra, Elvis, and the Beatles, right about Michael Jackson with the Jackson 5, Justin Timberlake with NSYNC, and Taylor Swift. They were the first on board in every one of those cases, before the critics got the point. Sometimes they mess up, as with Justin Bieber, but their track record is damn solid.

Massey kept telling me to hang on, to wait it out a few months or until the next fiscal year, but I thought it made more sense to see what Morris and Iovine were up to. I e-mailed Andy, basically saying, How about me? I got an e-mail right back: "This would be a great thing for us. I'm setting up a meeting with you and Jimmy." They flew me out to California on the same flight as Chris Kirkpatrick from NSYNC, just to remind me of this pop world I was now inhabiting (Chris is a sweet guy, actually, and offered to drive me to my hotel when I realized I didn't have my license with me). Interscope sent a car for me and whisked me to the Mondrian Hotel, home of the famous Skybar.

I met with Jimmy and Andy, and they explained in broad terms what was going to be called Jimmy and Doug's Farm Club (eventually shortened to Farmclub). This was going to be a multitiered thing involving the internet, a TV show, and a record label connected to Interscope. Unsigned artists would post their music online, some would be chosen to be profiled on a TV show (that's where I'd come in) that also would feature the hottest musical acts (a lot of them on Universal), and a few would get signed to a record deal. I think the term *synergy* was used more times in that meeting than I'd ever heard it before in my life cumulatively. And a lot of other terms that I was sort of familiar with: *broadband, upload, interactive*. It was so early in the internet game, but the idea was to get in quickly with something communal, build a pipeline to sign new music. They'd find artists in this new-tech way, and viewers and visitors to the website would be able to vote. It was sort of like buying a piece of property and then deciding what to build on it. It was virgin territory. It was before MySpace and PureVolume. Napster had only launched that June. The Wild West show triggered by file sharing was in its infancy, and no one knew how it all would shake out. Historically, new technology in the music business meant more money for record companies; that's how it worked from the time the 45 and 33⅓ records were invented, and up to cassettes and CDs. People bought new hardware, and you could sell them more music. I assume that's what Doug and Jimmy told the bigwigs at Universal: watch the cash roll in.

* * *

I thought I'd get around to figuring all that out, but for the time being it didn't matter, because all I would have to do was interview and introduce, and those things I already knew about. It sounded like fun. Andy said, "You're the right guy for this. This is a new venture and you have credibility. The artists will respect that you're involved, and it'll help brand Farmclub." I was in. I'd be hosting the show with someone else (ideally someone easier on the eyes), and be like a musical consultant for the Farmclub record label.

After the meeting, Andy drove me back to the Mondrian.

"So," I said, "you're going to fly me out here a few days a week for this?"

"A few days a week? You're fucking moving here."

Hmmm, okay . . . I guessed there was a big life change coming. To complicate my life even more, I was about to become a father again. I'd met Yvette two years earlier at a birthday party my friend Geordie Gillespie from Sony threw for me at China Grill; she'd tagged along with another friend, and we started going out. Two years later she became pregnant, while I was still at MTV before segueing into the Farmclub gig. There was a medical condition that could have threatened the baby, and Yvette needed good health care, so we decided to get married right away so she could get on my work insurance. I called my bosses at MTV to tell them, and we went down to city hall. To celebrate, we went to a funky soul-food restaurant in the East Village that I loved, Old Devil Moon, a real rock 'n' roll joint near Avenue A.

When the Farmclub gig came along, I didn't want to put Yvette through all the moving until I'd figured out where we were going to live, so we worked it out that she'd take the car and stay with her family in Florida, and I'd fly back and forth to see her in between shooting the show in LA and when I wasn't out in the field doing remote segments. Universal put me up temporarily in the Oakwood Apartments. Technically, everyone who stays at Oakwood is there temporarily. It's a housing complex for people in a transient state. During television pilot season, it's where families of aspiring actors from the flyover states take up residence. It's also where members of bands stay when they're cutting albums in LA, with the tab picked up by the record labels, money that the artists will never, ever recoup from record sales, so they wind up paying for it anyway. One morning, on parallel treadmills, it was me and members of Weezer, the Toadies, and Barenaked Ladies all trying to sweat out the toxins from the night before. During my stay, the community pool was very often a gathering spot for members of gangs from East LA who told building security, such as it was, that they were guests of Matt Pinfield. Some drug dealer or hip-hop artist with gang associations would meet me on the set of Farmclub, find out where I was staying, and tell all their friends that the place to be was at Pinfield's at Oakwood. So imagine a conglomeration of stage moms, rockers, and guys who might have had a role in the whole Tupac murder mystery sharing a pool deck. I'm going to pitch *Oakwood 2000* as a Showtime series.

One afternoon I brainstormed with Audrey Morrissey, one of the show's executive producers, and came up with the concept of doing personal segments on the new artists in their hometowns. We came up with the idea of the little backstory packages to let viewers know where these bands came from. Those bits I did for Farmclub were the predecessor of the canned segments on *American Idol* and every other talent show that followed. We did that first. Now Audrey is a producer on *The Voice*. We were first in a lot of ways, in fact, and were way ahead on trying to sync up television, music, and the internet. There was no streaming, no YouTube, none of that. People weren't even able to post video footage, only audio. And we had a staff of people listening to all these submissions. Winners were picked, and I'd show up at their front door in Kansas or somewhere like Ed McMahon with a check from Publishers Clearing House. Let's be honest: I loved the idea that not only was I going to meet young musicians and help them out, but I was going to travel to parts of the country that I never would have gone to otherwise. That was fun. Too much fun, sometimes. I'd get into a town like Mitchell, South Dakota, get fucked up, and end up singing Bad Company songs onstage in some cover band, along with whatever other songs they knew, even if I didn't always know the words that well. I'd eat at joints called the Steerhouse or the Cornhouse, go to rehearsals in basements, visit guys at their day jobs where they were making pizza. We took the camera crew to Nashville, Austin, Ft. Lauderdale, and Plymouth, Massachusetts.

I heard the birth of my second daughter over the phone. The doctor had to induce labor, and it simply couldn't wait, so I was at the Oakwoods in Burbank on March 3, 2000, when Maya was born. There were no camera phones then, no Skyping or FaceTime, so I just held the phone up to my ear. Maya's arrival was announced, fittingly, on MTV. Carson Daly was hosting *TRL*, and he said, "You know, I probably wouldn't be on radio or TV if it weren't for this guy, and I just wanted to say that Matt Pinfield and his wife had a baby today and her name is Maya." Later, Yvette's grandfather uploaded some pictures of Maya in the nursery and every-body at Farmclub gathered around a computer backstage at Universal Studios, and they all started cheering. The camera was right in tight on Maya's face, and she looked terrified.

What the Farmclub people did that was brilliant was buy the eleven o'clock hour on the USA Network on Monday nights. It may sound like a ratings graveyard, but it imme-diately followed the two strongest hours on cable televi-sion, WWF's *Raw*, at a peak of wrestling's popularity. That meant we had a built-in, heavily male, heavily young, heavily rock-inclined audience for our show. Plus, my cohost was going to be Ali Landry, who was Miss USA in 1996 and was bound to draw male eyeballs and make those eyeballs leap out of their sockets. That was the team, beauty and the beast, Monday nights. We had this perfect lead-in, and for our opening show we booked Dr. Dre, Eminem, 98 Degrees, and some female dance artist that we'd signed before the show launched. We were covering the hip-hop/boy-band bases that were the prime musical constituency in the fall of '99 when the show premiered. The ratings were killer, like a 15 share on a Monday night.

Almost immediately, our set became the hottest party in LA. Playboy Playmates were always hanging around. Jimmy Iovine's ex-wife, Vicki, had been a Playboy Playmate, and Jimmy was very shrewd. He knew Farmclub was going to be on after the WWF, and he figured, after watching two hours of sweaty dudes, guys would want to see some pretty girls. *Playboy* and Farmclub were a perfect fit, everyone agreed, especially me, and I was even happier about the association when I got a call from the production office: "We're going to send you a car to take you to Malibu and you're going to play volleyball with some Playmates." I know: and then I woke up. It was for real, and I almost didn't want to tell any of my friends about it, because what are they going to say? "Fuck you." Or maybe: "What beach?" A few weeks later, my assignment was to accompany a group of Playmates to go scuba diving off Catalina. "What did you do today?" "Oh, I went scuba diving with ten Playboy Playmates." It's unfair how good the Farmclub perks were, spending a day watching girls in tiny bikinis jump around in the sand pretending to play volleyball, all for a television bumper that might last thirty seconds.

Shooting all the location footage for the show was a blast. (Remember, this was in late '99, early 2000, when money in the music business was raining down so hard you just had to stand around with a bucket to catch it.) I'd go on the set for lavish hip-hop video shoots in Malibu mansions, open up a trailer door for an interview, and see my subject lying on the floor with a bottle of Cristal and two extras who were probably hired the night before in the VIP room at Jumbo's Clown Room.

I was flown to Miami to do a piece on Sisqo's "Thong Song." It hadn't been released yet, but we were tipped to it by the people at Def Soul, a new Universal label. That's where I was, at the Sisqo shoot, the first time I saw Farmclub on TV, October 1999. I was so pumped after watching it, and I went out to hit the South Beach clubs, thinking, I'm going to have some drinks and fucking go wild. I thought I'd hitched a ride on the next big thing on TV, a show that could be for the new century what MTV was in the '80s and '90s, the spot where all the hot elements of pop culture converge. Sometimes you feel as though it's the right moment, and that's how it felt that night *Farmclub* premiered and I was out on the town in Miami Beach, being embraced by the hip-hop guys and gorgeous South Beach girls and being confronted by Christina Aguilera because she'd heard Fred Durst had "been talking shit" about her, which wasn't true, at least not to me. A picture of me and Christina from that encounter ended up in *Ocean Drive* magazine.

Where there's music and girls (and drugs), there's going to be a scene. Musicians who weren't booked to play the show dropped by to check it out. Tommy Lee came by the same night Scott Weiland did, and Scott said to him, "Man, I've always wanted to meet you." Tommy said, "Yeah, me too. I think we've been in front of some of the same judges."

Everybody turned up, the guys from Rancid and Smash Mouth, whoever was in town. Nothing was ever officially announced, and those were the days before you could let everyone know what was happening with texts and tweets, so it was old-fashioned word of mouth, one person calling another, "Hey, *Farmclub* is shooting tonight with Primus." It was a show you wanted to play on, and a set that was pure insanity. We had an N.W.A reunion one night, and they had to get someone to sub for Eazy-E. Snoop Dog said he'd do it, but we couldn't get him out of the dressing room because he was so smoked up. Dre, Jimmy, and Andy were all standing around outside, waiting for Snoop to emerge. The performance went great, and at one point I was standing next to Quentin Tarantino and he said, "I fucking feel like a kid again!" He was running around the set, so excited to see N.W.A back together. Will.i.am was just signed to Interscope with the Black Eyed Peas before Fergie joined them, and he was always there. Dre and Eminem invited me over to the studio, and I went out and bought a Thin Lizzy album for Dre to listen to, because I thought it'd be cool for him to sample the bass line from the cut "Showdown." He only knew "The Boys Are Back in Town," but he was open to checking it out.

One of the many cool things about Farmclub was that it acknowledged the strong affinity between hard rock and hip-hop. When we put together a CD from the show, it was like, Limp Bizkit with Method Man; it opened with N.W.A and Eminem; it had Staind and Nickelback. Artists would meet up at the tapings and start talking about doing projects together. We didn't care if someone watching the show who liked Eve might not be into No Doubt or LL Cool J, or if an Incubus fan dug Lil' Kim. We never expected everyone would be equally into everything, but we wanted to show what was going on in modern music. Like Jay-Z with Memphis Bleek and Beanie Sigel doing "Do It Again," Outkast doing "Ms. Jackson," U2 doing "Beautiful Day." Those were some classic performances. We got away with a lot on the show: Eminem wanted to come on with the group D12, a hip-hop act on his Shady label. He was one of the biggest artists in the world, and on the Interscope roster, so what he wanted he got, and I had to say, on (basic-cable) television, "Here's D12 with 'I Shit on You.'" I'm so proud of bleepable moments like that.

Not everyone is a fan of rap-influenced rock, but it was an undeniable force, and I can't understand why a segment of the rock world gets ticked off whenever a hip-hop artist is being considered for induction into the Rock and Roll Hall of Fame. Any rock hall that wouldn't recognize the rock attitude in Public Enemy, N.W.A, and the Beastie Boys has a very narrow definition of the genre. Farmclub caught and documented a moment in the history of music when barriers were breaking down. Take someone like Kid Rock, who was breaking big by combining elements of rock and hip-hop, and southern rock and country. He can headline rock festivals or country festivals like Stagecoach. He can show up onstage with the Allman Brothers Band to do old Marshall Tucker Band songs, or duet with Miranda Lambert. Even I got to sing live with him once, at a giant racetrack show in Phoenix in front of sixty thousand people; Joe C., the little person who'd rev up the crowd at Kid Rock shows, was ill one night, and I filled in on "Devil without a Cause." Joe C.'s part of the song went "I'm three foot tall with a ten-foot prick," and I had to change that to "I'm five six, bald, with a ten-foot prick." The lights went up during my part, and the crowd went berserk.

No expense was spared on *Farmclub*'s production. We shot on Stage 42 at Universal in Studio City—it looked like a set for *The Matrix*—and there was catering for a mile, sushi, wet bars, and giant TV screens everywhere. People were getting hammered. I was usually working, in my dressing room prepping, out front hosting, or doing an interview on the set. One female acquaintance of Tommy Lee's came up to me backstage and said, "I'm going to put my hands down your pants and jerk you off and no one's going to know it." I said, Yeah, everyone's going to know it, because my bosses and Ali are sitting right there on the couch, and anyway, I'm married. A rumor swirled that two of the girls were 69ing on one of the appetizer tables, and since it's Universal Studios, the lot was corralled by tourist trains, and visitors got more of a behind-the-scenes glimpse than they'd anticipated. Women were always running around half naked. Gang members were having arguments about who got to sell blow to the performers. Craven Moorehead (yeah,

I know: subtle), a porn director, would show up and pass around copies of his DVDs. It was mayhem. One visitor on the Universal tour complained that she, her grandmother, and her six-year-old kid witnessed some form of debauchery, and finally we got the word that alcohol was banned. Like alcohol was the biggest problem. As much as I could drink, the time I got the most paralyzed was smoking weed with Method Man and Redman. It was some kind of hydroponic stuff.

In mid-2000 the *New York Times* touted our ratings (the number-three show on the network among young males, behind only the wrestling franchise, and "clobbering MTV head-to-head"), our production values ("superior sound, a thrust stage within touching distance of the audience and the authentic feel of a live performance"), and the way we were bridging "old and new media." All we needed was time to catch up with us. But we were derailed by a combination of things. The WWF left USA for TNN, depriving us of their lead-in audience; the dot-com boom of the '90s was skidding to the wall, and music-related start-ups were hit hard. And Universal, looking at the bottom line, saw that for all the cultural inroads we were making, *Farmclub* wasn't yet reaping profitable crops. As well as the TV show was doing in its time slot, not enough people were up to speed on the whole broadband-download side for the website to have any real resonance. In April 2001, *Farmclub* went off the air.

Three years later, I was hosting the U2 radio special for *How to Dismantle an Atomic Bomb*, an Interscope album, and Jimmy Iovine was there for the taping. He came up to me afterward, told me I did a great job with U2, and then he brought up Farmclub and said, "We were just too early."

Encounters:
U2

Dublin, 2000

I'm in Ireland to interview U2, in advance of their album *All That You Can't Leave Behind*. They've given me a copy of the album to listen to—on CD (this is before iPods)—and I pop it in my Discman. I remember walking out of my hotel and going on a stroll through the streets of Dublin, listening to that album for the first time. No one had heard the album yet, just the band and a few people at their record label. I'll never forget it, hearing that intro to "Beautiful Day." What a fucking moment, one of those times where I said, What an amazing life I'm getting to live. Here I am in Dublin, where my ancestors are from, and I'm here with one of the biggest bands in the world, and I know that soon everyone in the world is going to hear this music.

I go to the studio to talk to Bono and the Edge, and I'm sitting on the couch. I pull up the blinds, and there's the bog the band was standing on in the "Gloria" video. I got chills.

In 1980, I was at a record store, as usual. I bought a lot of records on impulse. I saw this single, "A Day without Me," on Island Records from the UK, and I didn't know anything about U2, but I loved the cover because it looked very stark, and I loved that post-punk, sort of depressing rock. I bought it blind and brought it home, and I was hooked by the Edge's echoey guitar and Bono's voice, the introspective lyrics. I liked that kind of shit.

When the import copy of *Boy* came out, it had a shirtless young boy on the cover, and that's why Island didn't use that image. They thought it was pedophile-like, so instead they used a stretched-out picture of the band, a silhouettish photo. I loved that album, and then "I Will Follow" came out, and by that time I was playing it on the radio and spinning it at the clubs, and as soon as I put it on people would jam the dance floor.

So then U2 were coming in to play the Fast Lane in Asbury Park, and my friends and I would drive down. I brought my tape recorder. They played "I Will Follow" twice in their set; they didn't have that many songs then. Afterward, the band wanted to come out and talk to people. Nobody's fighting to get backstage to see U2, they're just a bunch of young kids from Dublin. I went up to Bono and the Edge after the show and I said, "Guys, you were great." I told them that I'd bought their records, and that I was a DJ at a college station. Is it okay if I get an ID from you?

An enthusiastic, young, high-pitched voice goes, "Hi. I'm Bono. I'm the singer in a band from Dublin called U2, and you're listening to WRUS-FM, Rutgers University."

That was my first encounter with U2.

They became one of the key bands for commercial alternative stations, and mainstream rock radio was warming up to them. This was the period where I was still at the radio station at the shore, doing weekends at the other station, and I went to see all their shows, but I didn't end up reconnecting with U2 until around seven, eight years later, in the summer of 1993, the Zoo TV tour.

My friend Steve Leeds from Island Records invited me over to Ireland. He wanted me to see this band called the Frames, who had some members who were from the movie *The Commitments*. And I'd become friendly with the guys in the UK band the Wonder Stuff, who were playing a big homecoming show in Birmingham. Also, we were going to see U2 play a huge stadium show in Cork.

We were going to fly from Dublin to Cork, which isn't very far, but U2 had their own private jet, ZooAir92. They had these flight attendants who had these red T-shirts that just said *WOW*.

At the venue, we were seated in the president's box. It's me and Steve, and Adam Clayton's brother, and Prime Minister Ahern and his family. I'm right behind the prime minister when Bono starts going off about Ireland's laws about contraception, how people were being arrested for selling condoms. I just looked at Adam's brother and said, "Holy shit." First of all, it's bizarre enough that we're in this private box with the prime minister, and now Bono is bringing all this up in front of like fifty thousand people at the Páirc Uí Chaoimh.

Fast-forward a few years to early 1998, the band's PopMart tour. Now I'm hosting *120 Minutes*. I'm invited to go to Brazil for U2's first South American show ever. We were staying at the same hotel as the band. The flight is on the Viacom jet, with a few other people—Tom Freston, the head of MTV; Bill Flanagan, U2's biographer; Jeff Pollack, an MTV/VH1 consultant. We get on the plane at Teterboro and have to make a stop in Barbados to pick up Paul McGuinness, U2's manager, and to refuel. Flanagan and Freston, all those guys, want to go to this square in Bahia, the City of Drummers, where Paul Simon shot the video for "The Obvious Child."

I'm pretty hammered from drinking the native drinks. This crazy bald fucker, standing to the side. The locals kept pushing the tourists around and pickpocketing them. Freston had his glasses stolen. Flanagan's wallet was lifted. We go down to the Turismo Policía and it's just this long line of white people who were robbed at the center. So much for the rhythm of the saints. I'm sure Paul Simon never just went wandering around the square by himself. I look at Bill. "I hate to say it, but I don't think you're getting your wallet back."

Eventually, we got out of there and flew to Rio. All of us were put up in the nicest hotel, the Copacabana.

That night, Bono and I got dysentery. I was eating fried fish and boiled vegetables. And I thought the water in the bathroom was drinkable. So I was asking for it. After dinner, we all went out to have drinks at this carnival. So the next morning, I was sick and hungover, and I get a call: "Matt, we're going to the venue early, and we're taking helicopters." I got on one of those helicopters where you can see under your feet, and I thought my balls were in my throat. We flew over that famous giant statue in Rio, Christ the Redeemer, going at high speed. I was scared shitless, thought I was going to die.

We landed at the Autódromo Internacional Nelson Piquet, this big racetrack in Rio. For "Desire," Brazilian percussionists were added to amp up the song's already riveting rhythms, and the band threw in a piece of Van Morrison's "Gloria." The VIP section we were in was just a platform, and around three quarters of the way through the show, it started to collapse. I could tell that Bono wasn't feeling well—he got the same bug I did—and I don't think he was onstage for the last encore, "Wake Up Dead Man." In any case, he was too ill to do the interview later back at the hotel.

U2 had requested that they not be interviewed by Brazil's MTV guys. They wanted me to do it, and for MTV Brazil to use the footage. Since Bono was recuperating, it was me, the Edge, Larry, and Adam, and I swear I did the greatest interview I've ever done with U2. We went through every album from start to finish. From those early albums I loved, *Boy*, *October*, *War*, all the way up to *Pop*, the whole story, going into detail about every record, even more obscure songs like "Hold Me, Thrill Me, Kiss Me, Kill Me." For a U2 fan, it's mind-blowing. We had the greatest time; the guys said they loved it. A week later, we found out that the MTV Brazil guys lost half of the fuckin' footage. Freston was so pissed. I was too, and I was still feeling the effects of the Rio trip—I weighed ten pounds less when I got back to New York. But I don't need the recorded evidence of that conversation. In my memory, it's a beautiful day.

Encounters:
KISS

Los Angeles, 1998

"Hey, listen, it's Gene. Look, why don't you come to KISS headquarters and finish up this voiceover, and then I'll take you to lunch?"

Simmons and the band had asked me to do some narration for a KISS documentary, and there were some lines that didn't sync up with the visuals. I was going to reread the script at their studio. It was an easy gig, maybe seven or eight lines.

Gene came and got me in his Lincoln Navigator and drove me to record the lines, and then we went to a cool steakhouse in LA.

When we were driving back he said, "You want to come to rehearsal?"

Uh . . . YEAH!

"Dude, you do know everything about the music, don't you?" Because we were talking about the English band the Move, who'd been a big influence on KISS, and he was surprised how knowledgeable I was about their catalog.

"Not that I thought your reputation was bullshit, but . . . I'm impressed with you."

"It's because I love the music."

It seems so obvious to me that the more you care about

something, the more you want to dig inside it, but people are always commenting on the rock data I have in my head and can rattle off.

We pulled up to this place called Cole Rehearsal Studios, one of the three main rehearsal spaces in LA, along with Swing House and S.I.R. Gene, you know he's tight with a dollar, he wasn't going to waste any money, so as huge as KISS were, they were booked into the smallest room. Audioslave, who were called Citizen at the time, had the big room. Gene and I pulled into the parking lot, and Peter Criss and Ace Frehley were just standing there across the lot.

"Where the fuck have you been, man?"

"Fuck you, I was taking Pinfield to lunch."

"All right, where's Paul?" Stanley hadn't shown up for rehearsal yet. We went inside, waiting for him, and in the meantime they started doing costume fittings for the upcoming Psycho Circus tour. A guy comes in with these outfits, classic KISS gear from like the *Love Gun* era. And Gene goes, "Put my boots on."

I'm like a half-foot shorter than Gene, maybe. So my leg buckles, and I almost break an ankle.

"Gene, holy shit."

"Imagine walking around in those for two and a half hours a night."

Still no Paul. We're sitting around.

"You gotta check out my new bass amp." He puts a quarter on the tom-tom drum, hits that bass, and says, "Listen to that resonate." While I'm listening to that, I walk around to where the mic stand is for the lead vocals, and there's a set list of the songs they were going to run through.

"Oh, all the classics. Not too many new songs."

"So you like the list?"

"Gene, I used to sing these songs in a band when I was fifteen."

"You wanna have a go?"

"Fuck, yeah. Let's do it!"

"What song do you want to do?"

I mentioned "Coming Home," from *Hotter Than Hell,* which is one of my favorites. Very Beatlesque. But Ace didn't remember it. How about "Rock Bottom"? It's on *Dressed to Kill,* and also on *Alive!* I love the song.

I did the whole song. I fucking killed it.

Gene says, "I can't believe how good your voice is, how much control you have. You don't sing like you talk at all. What else do you want to do?"

Then Peter Criss, who's behind me, goes, "Do 'Do You Love Me.'"

And that was one of the most surreal moments. Imagine having three of the original members of KISS playing with you, and the entire first verse of that song is just you and the drummer. I sing the verse through the PA with no musicians or backing vocals, and then all of a sudden Gene and Ace come in, and I'm doing Paul's parts, and at that moment it's like I'm thirteen again, and I'm listening to KISS with my headphones on, except now it's not in my headphones, it's the actual guys around me. And one of them says, "How about a third song?"

"How about 'A Hundred Thousand Years'?" On the *Alive!* album, there's a major drum solo in the middle of the song, and a crowd call-and-response thing. So we get to that point in the breakdown, and Gene looks at me, and I go, "Studio version! Studio version!" Like, I'm not going to do the ten-minute live thing.

We finished, and the band was all pumped up.

"Do you want to do any more?"

I didn't want to overstay my welcome, so I left the mic and sat down, and then they ran through "Deuce," and it's like their energy level dropped in half. Because, you know, they've done the song thousands and thousands of times. And Ace looked over at me and said . . .

"You know what, man? You should come sing with us more often. It lit a fire under our ass."

The thing about KISS that a lot of people don't realize is that Gene and Paul were the biggest fans of Anglo rock. They would listen to Scott Muni's "Things from England" on his WNEW-FM radio show every Friday afternoon. They were obsessed with English glam: Slade, T. Rex, Bowie, anything that had that three-minute Beatles-ish thing. They loved the Move, with Roy Wood and Jeff Lynne, and their song "Fire Brigade." Their whole idea was to make those kinds of pop songs that resembled the music they loved. They used the Beatles' blueprint. Nobody is the Beatles, but I think that's commendable, whether you were a fan or not.

You have to explain the whole KISS thing to people. I realize that. They never got big pats on the back from the rock press, and they aren't taken seriously. For years, the industry heavyweights who sit on the board of the Rock and Roll Hall of Fame wanted nothing to do with KISS, and there's always been talk about an official blackballing of the band. It wasn't until 2013 that the band finally gained admission, and that was largely due to Tom Morello from Rage Against the Machine. Tom's been playing guitar with Springsteen's E Street Band recently, and he let it be known to Bruce that KISS was a big reason that he picked up a guitar. It happens that Springsteen's manager Jon Landau is one of the key decision makers for the slate of nominees. Sometimes it just takes a push in the right direction.

As a kid, you don't make distinctions between rock that's

hip and rock that isn't. All I cared about was the sound and the image. Songs like "Detroit Rock City," about a guy getting drunk and being killed in a highway accident—that was so visual and cinematic to me. They were like cartoon superheroes, and their songs were about the rock life. Picture an impressionable twelve-year-old boy, just figuring out how to masturbate, hearing these songs about girls and rock 'n' rolling all nite and wondering, "What does this mean? Can I live this life? Can I touch this?" They were in another dimension, and all you knew about them was what you could figure out by looking at the album covers and reading articles about them in *Circus*, *Creem*, and *Hit Parader*.

I mean, there was definitely a period where the band jumped the shark for me. I wanted music that dug deeper. But later on, through the lens of nostalgia, I went back to those first four albums. The music that grips you when you're on the precipice of sexual awareness, that sticks with you no matter what.

Years later, after the band had changed personnel quite a bit and weren't on the mainstream radar as much, I was at MTV, and Alex Coletti, who was the producer of all the *Unplugged* shows, came into my office.

"Why doesn't your music department want to do a *KISS Unplugged*? You're the only guy in this place that appreciates KISS. Can you explain it to them?"

I walked down the hallway into Patti Galluzzi's office.

"What's up?"

"Listen, KISS are worthy of an *Unplugged* gig. I can break it down in numbers. It may not be your favorite band, but I need to tell you, every record sells around a half a million copies with no promotion at all, so if only a third of those people tune in the first night it airs, that's like almost two hundred thousand fans."

"You know? I think you're right."

At that point, KISS was Gene and Paul and two other guys. They'd gone through all their drugs and craziness and replaced Peter and Ace, and everyone, including me, expected that it would be the new edition of KISS for the *Unplugged* show. To older fans like me, the real KISS is the original four members, the classic lineup, but they hadn't played together in years.

I went to the first *Unplugged* rehearsal, and Ace and Peter walked in, yelling, "Hey, you motherfuckers." After three or four songs at the taping, they brought them on, and the place went berserk. Look, everyone knows that Paul and especially Gene are all about the business, the KISS brand. It's a cut-and-dried thing with them, which I respect. And this *Unplugged* shot did so much to rebrand them. It led to a full-scale reunion.

To thank us, Gene and Peter took me and Alex Coletti out to lunch.

"You were the guys that got this thing done," Gene said. It was so meaningful to me that I played a part in getting this band back together. At the lunch, I talked nonstop about those first two KISS albums, and the next thing that happened was I got a call from Gene. "We'd really like you to narrate our new documentary. You're a part of why it happened, and you should be the voice of the doc. I'll give you two grand."

Typical Gene.

"Dude, you're going to make like a ton. At least give me five grand." (I wasn't being paid that much at MTV either, so I could use the cash.)

He said okay, and that he was going to send me the videotapes and the script, and I thought, "Wait a minute, let me do the math. Five grand means I have to rent a studio and do the voiceover?" I didn't tell Gene, but in between *TRL* and *120 Minutes* I would go into the vocal booth at MTV. They threw on a

DAT (digital audio tape) as a favor to me, and I read the script. But because I wasn't synching it to the video, the timings were off. I sent the first one to the band.

"There are about thirty-seven lines that don't match up with the video."

"Really? How'd that happen?" All innocent.

I did them again at MTV, and this time they're like, everything is great, but there are still seven lines that don't work.

And because I fucked up those seven lines, and had to redo them in LA, and because Paul Stanley decided not to show up at rehearsal that same day, I fulfilled a quarter-century-old fantasy of singing lead for KISS. Isn't that crazy?

My Brilliant A&R Career
(or: As the Industry Crumbles)

This was what was going on: in an opulent tower of a building smack in the middle of Manhattan, Madison Avenue and Fifty-fifth Street, the titans at Columbia Records and their parent company, Sony Music, were behaving as though they were rulers of an invincible empire. In a way, they were. Columbia Records was the longest-standing record company on the planet, and it was still raking in the cash: Destiny's Child, John Mayer, Train, and other young acts were generating sales heat, and there was no reason to think things would crumble. Unless you were actually paying attention. Because in 1999, Shawn Fanning had launched a little enterprise called Napster, and that would wind up causing a few small problems. But all that wouldn't catch up with the Sony executives for a few years. When I was approached by Columbia Records in 2001 to become an A&R guy, I thought it was an incredible shot at doing something rewarding and meaningful. A&R—it stands for "Artists and Repertoire"—is the process of identifying and developing talent and being the creative liaison between artist and record company, and it was the next logical move for me, working the system from within, as they say. I'd already struck up friendships with A&R people at Sony's label Epic, which boasted bands like Pearl Jam, Rage Against the Machine, Silverchair, and Oasis. Epic was like Columbia's kid-brother label in the Sony system, but at that time, Epic was kicking Columbia's ass in rock music. Columbia had Alice in Chains, and heritage bands like Aerosmith and Bruce Springsteen and the E Street Band, but their rock roster needed a jolt of new energy. That's where I would come in. At least that's how the idea was pitched to me by the people at Sony and Columbia who were wooing me to join the A&R team.

I loved hanging out with people like Goldstone and Massey, people who loved music, talking about it and making it, and I'd made no secret that A&R was something I wanted to take a crack at someday. When I was at MTV and Farmclub, during this fertile, brilliant period, I thought about what it might be like to work with bands from the very earliest stages, help them find their sound, work with them on their live presentation, watch them develop, and hang their platinum albums on my office wall. And going to work at Sony would also mean going back to New York City. I'd liked having the space in LA, having a guest house filled with all my records and shit, being able to walk my kid around the canyons. But when Farmclub fell apart, I was uncertain what the next phase would be. In the back of my mind, I thought I'd go back east. Then I heard from Columbia.

Getting the call from Columbia Records was like getting called up to the majors. Columbia was the label of Dylan and Springsteen and Leonard Cohen. The Byrds, Paul Revere and the Raiders, and the Cyrkle. Some of the first singles that marked my childhood had Columbia's vivid red "walking eye" insignia. Columbia was Big Red. It was Big Brother and the Holding Company, Moby Grape, and Santana. You'd walk down the Columbia halls at 550 Madison Avenue and see photos of Miles Davis, Tony Bennett, Johnny Cash, Billie Holiday. Robert Johnson! Columbia's John Hammond had compiled and released Johnson's *King of the Delta Blues Singers,* one of the most significant albums in the history of blues (and, by extension, rock). If I went to work there, the Columbia brand would be on any album I had a hand in making. What could possibly be more prestigious?

I was talking to my friend Steve Kingston one day. He had programmed Z-100 in New York City, the nation's biggest pop station, and was now at K-Rock. I told him things were over at Farmclub, and he pitched me to his friend Don Ienner at Columbia. So I got a meeting with Ienner and with Will Botwin in the Sony building.

I got on the elevator at ground level and took it up to 550 Madison's lobby in the sky, which led to another elevator bank and the label offices. On the top floor, thirty-five, there was a private executive dining room, and a separate room that just served sushi (Sony was a Japanese-owned company, after all), and an area with a piano that artists like Alicia Keys sometimes played at their Columbia auditions. The view was spectacular, facing north across Central Park. The sushi was amazing, by the way.

Don Ienner could really turn on a sales pitch. He was like a motivational speaker crossed with a college football coach. People were genuinely terrified of him. But he could also lay on the flattery and be charming as hell. He told me he'd followed my career, read about me in *Rolling Stone,* knew that people gave a shit about what I had to say about music. He said he knew that bands (like Columbia's Alice in Chains and Aerosmith) respected me. One idea he threw at me was putting together a kind of supergroup of members of the various Seattle bands. I thought that was an intriguing idea, but I was much more excited about finding new artists and building things from scratch. Also in my initial Columbia meeting was Will Botwin, who had managed acts like Los Lobos, John Hiatt, and Lyle Lovett. I knew Will's creative sensibility would be a match for what I wanted to do as an A&R guy.

I went to Florida to get my daughter, then flew back to LA and waited while my contract was negotiated. I got a phone call from Will. "Look, either you can stay in Los Angeles and be a consultant, with no insurance or benefits, or you can move back to New York and we'll make you senior director of A&R, part of the staff, and if things are going well, we'll promote you to vice president after the first period." That was the offer, a two-year contract with the option for a third, and it wasn't that close a call for me: I needed to take the New York position, have health insurance and all that. I had a one-year-old kid to care for. Sign me up.

Before I left LA, I had breakfast with Steve Perry from Journey at this tiny place on Victory Boulevard. He gave me a crash course in Columbia, and on Don Ienner in particular. He said, "You're going to work at Columbia. I used to get mad at Donnie when I would play him music and he'd say, 'Where's the single?' I was so fucking offended. Fuck, I've been doing this a long time. Don't ask me about the fucking single. But then I found a band that I wanted to develop, and I found myself channeling Donnie: 'Where's the fucking single?' It's funny, when you're on the other side, you see things from the other perspective." In A&R, the biggest question was, how is this going to work? Meaning, of course, how are we going to make money on this? I never had to think about whether the bands I loved and supported and played on the air were making money for their labels. That was without question the least important factor to me; it never even occurred to me. Now it was something I had to think about all the time.

I worried a bit about forming bonds with artists I wanted to work with, becoming close friends with them—that had been a big part of why I was successful on the radio and TV, because of my ability to develop a personal rapport—and then having to be the voice of the record company, driven by the interests of Columbia. I grappled with the idea, and there were senior people at Sony who would tell me, "Don't make friends with the bands. They aren't your friends." I knew what they meant, not to let my personal feelings cloud my judgment, but it was such a reversal from the world I knew. One of the first A&R people at Columbia who introduced himself to me when I showed up for work in July 2001 was Kevin Patrick. He was checking out a rock band called Hot Action Cop; a few labels were circling. He asked me if I wanted to fly down to Nashville to see them play and meet them. Kevin is a record geek like I am, and we spent about three hours at the Great Escape record store in Nashville going through boxes of 45s. He said to me, "There are going to be good days and bad days, and you're going to have a front-row seat for all of it." He was right about that.

At the time, I was super optimistic. I had no idea what was in store for me. For one thing, I was now in the position of having to defend and justify my musical taste. When I was on the radio and at MTV, I followed my instincts, and that was that. And I was the one who people tried to convince: play my record, see my band, air my video. I'd be given the whole hype routine because I had the power to make things happen. Walking into Columbia was an entirely new game. At meetings we'd gather in a conference room and the tone would be, "What have you got?" One by one, we—some of the top A&R talent in the industry as far as I was concerned—would pop in a demo, or play a video, and talk about the artist or the band we were interested in signing, make our case: this band is starting to cause some commotion in this market, this track is getting some airplay in this market. Today, A&R is mostly research: you can go on the internet and see what's going on. This band has this many Facebook followers, this many hits on YouTube. It's all statistically verifiable. Back in 2001, 2002, we didn't have that kind of information, not yet. It was still a mostly instinctive process: Does this song sound like a hit? Does this video show any star quality? Those A&R meetings could be nerve-racking. Don Ienner was not easy to please, and his displeasure was not easy to endure. His criticism could be withering. And once you got over the hurdle and got his seal of approval, if he could read enthusiasm in the room (the A&R men and women were supportive of each other, but were always candid), then you had to go through the major-label obstacle course: making the album, identifying the lead tracks, getting the promotion team jazzed up, finding a place in the release schedule of the biggest record company in the world. It took a while for me to get the hang of it. My previous gigs were about what I liked. This one was about what I could prove.

On one of my trips to Jacksonville, Florida, I heard a song on a local music show by a band called Ten High, later called Trouble Is, and finally, Start Trouble. I thought they had energy, attitude, and terrific songs written by their front man, Luke Walker. I suppose you could call them a punk-pop band, more or less in the same genre as Weezer and Blink-182. One of their songs ("Chemical") had a line, "Love is a chemical straight from your genitals." They also had a song called "Let's Get Fucked Up." This wasn't the most sophisticated stuff, but a lot of it cracked me up in an adolescent way. I thought they were funny. It was really Luke's project; he'd done these tracks as demos, using loops in place of other musicians, and it was one of those demos, the one with "Chemical," that I played in our A&R meeting and that got them signed to Columbia. For a producer I hired John Travis, an English guy who was influenced by some of the bands I worshipped (Thin Lizzy, T. Rex). He'd worked on cool hip-hop records as an engineer, and produced Kid Rock. I was happy with the album, *Every Solution Has Its Problem*, and delivered it to the label, the first album that I'd shepherded start to finish. All I had to do was let the formidable Columbia Records machine do its thing.

The problem was, the release schedule was crammed with surefire records, and I had to wait my turn. During the "let's wait" time, the sound of alternative radio shifted, as it always does. You can't make records for "now," because by the time everything is done, "now" is something else. Columbia delayed the release of the Start Trouble album for too long. What might have worked in 2002 was a bit dated in 2004, when bands like the Strokes and the White Stripes were moving the modern rock format. The promotion department wanted to work the song "Non Stop" at radio, but the senior guys insisted on "Chemical," and when that track stalled out, game over. I learned an incredibly valuable lesson about the politics of life at a major label: bad timing can fuck everything up. And another lesson: you need total support from the company or else you're going to get lost. Columbia loved the idea that I was still doing radio—I'd landed a slot on Sunday nights doing a show called the Buzz on the number-one alternative station in America, K-Rock in New York—but I couldn't ethically have any say in whether Columbia records got played on the air. I tried everything to save Start Trouble, going in and doing remixes, doing a "clean" edit of "Chemical," but finally Donnie and Will basically shrugged it all off, Promotion moved on to other priorities, and my record died on the vine.

As an A&R person, when you're trying to convince an artist to sign with you, it's about establishing trust. You have a job and a steady paycheck and an expense account, and maybe this is one of a handful of bands you'll work with. The artist has one career, and he or she is putting it in your hands, trusting that what you say is for real; that you'll be an advocate and watch over every phase of the project. It's a big commitment and there's so much at stake. Sometimes, for the band, absolutely everything is at stake. Bands who make failed debut albums often never get another shot. You will— at least for a while—and the label has a big roster to worry about and bank on. But the band is back to the basement, and the dream of someday headlining at Madison Square Garden or Wembley Stadium is over for good.

I received a five-song demo from a Seattle-based band called Acceptance. I listened, and immediately called the band's manager, Jonathan Daniel. "We've got to make this happen." It caught me from the moment I heard the introduction to the song "Permanent," the sheer velocity and force of it. Jason Vena's vocals cut through me, and I thought the group had the potential to be as big as Soundgarden and STP. I was facing heavy competition, so I needed to move fast. I got Columbia to bring the band to New York for a private showcase, and that sealed it. We licensed the five original demos, and two live songs, to an indie, which released a debut EP. It was all about getting the word out and building a reputation ahead of the first full-length Columbia album, which took a little too much time; *Phantoms* didn't come out until almost two years after the EP. I don't know how to explain this, except that there was all this corporate scrambling going on at the time. We had heated discussions over what direction to take the band, whether to release "Permanent" or "Different" as the lead track, whether to go with the original version or to re-record. Everybody interfering. Everyone with a different opinion.

Sony—the whole music business, really—had undergone a lot of changes by the time I signed Acceptance in 2003. No one in the executive offices at the label could get a grip on how to keep riding on the rampaging mechanical bull that technology was turning the industry into. Desperate to control the uncontrollable effects of internet-music-sharing, and to keep customers purchasing music, Sony along with other record labels launched the New Coke of the music industry: the DualDisc. Part CD, part DVD, altogether klutzy, and not playable on all CD and DVD players. Another fiasco was XCP, or Extended Copy Protection, which, in trying to keep people from duplicating the music, had the wonderful result of infecting computers trying to, you know, *play the music*. The debut by Acceptance was one of the unfortunate albums stained by the XCP tattoo. There were lawsuits, and recalls of product, and eventual discontinuation, but millions of CDs were infected. It was the stupidest thing, this attempt to stop pirating, because a kid buys an Acceptance CD, he's going to want to put the music on his iPod, right? XCP makes that impossible. Music is all about peer-to-peer experience, discovering a band and sharing it. If this type of technology had existed when I was a teenager, and I could have shared the music I bought, made copies for my friends, rode my bike around with an iPod-like device in my pocket, what would have made me happier than that?

All these factors came into play, label delays and indecision, corporate mishaps, and it sucked.

Acceptance's debut was barely marketed or promoted, and it still sold more than a hundred thousand copies and got great reviews from the hard rock press. One review ended with the line, "This band will be huge unless Columbia fucks it up."

The rewards of A&R are so high when it's working, but the odds against success are even higher, and you wind up making promises that you're not able to keep. You want to believe in the label. You want to believe that the planets will align and everything will work out. That was the naïveté of it for me, because I thought everyone was going to understand my passion and work real hard and do the right thing. I went to Jason Vena's wedding, and I knew he was frustrated, and I understood. *Phantoms* should have been huge. So many bands, some famous, some not, have told me that the Acceptance album was a template for them when they started out. Jason didn't want for money; his family owned a car dealership, and he was going to be fine financially. But it was heartbreaking to him. We felt that if Columbia had worked harder and longer, they could have kept building on those hundred thousand sales. "Different" was taken to alternative radio, and there's a nice video of it, but it was more of a pop song, like Train's "Drops of Jupiter," and that's what Columbia did best, swing for the fences with the most "commercial" track. It's a favorite of mine from the album, but it wasn't completely indicative of the stuff the kids loved. I'm not bitter about what happened with Start Trouble or Acceptance, just disappointed; I got to swing the bat a bunch of times, and had the chance to sign a lot of bands. We picked up distribution of a California band called A Static Lullaby, who were signed to Ferret Records and had a cool track, "The Shooting Star That Destroyed Us."

Columbia screwed up the Killradio situation in typical record-label fashion. A station in LA, Indie1031, was starting to generate some noise in the market. They were giving K-Rock some competition. Killradio was booked to play an Indie1031 show, with the clear understanding that the station would bang the fuck out of "Do You Know?" to promote the gig. Then Columbia said, no, we're going to cancel that show and try and see if we can get K-Rock to play the record. We pulled the band, 1031 rightfully says, fuck you, fuck your band, no more airplay here. K-Rock never played it, the relationship with 1031 was done, the song was dead.

I got thrown some wacky assignments at Columbia. One, which could be construed as a form of punishment, was to go through the entire recorded catalog—something like twenty-five full-length cassettes—of Mary-Kate and Ashley Olsen, just to make sure the track listings on the packaging matched the music. I think we were in the process of transferring these songs for CD release. As soon as I heard one lyric from each song and determined it was, indeed, the words to "I Am the Cute One," "Pool Party," or "What's

All the Noise About Boys?," I could move on confidently to the next track. I should have called my attorney to see if this fell under the category of unfair labor practices, but I was a good Sony soldier.

Another wild project I worked on was an album called *Forcible Entry*, a World Wrestling Federation compilation album of bands doing wrestlers' entrance themes. Some tracks were remixes, like Rob Zombie's "Never Gonna Stop (The Black Cat Crossing Mix)," Marilyn Manson's "The Beautiful People (The WWF Remix)," and Limp Bizkit's "Rollin' (Dead Man Mix)." I also reached out to Creed and asked them if we could have a cut that had only been on an English B-side, "Young Grow Old." It wasn't an easy sell for some bands, because Vince McMahon and the WWF wanted publishing rights to all the material. If they were wrestling fans, or they were younger bands who thought it was good exposure, they'd sign off, but some of the bands' managers took issue. It was definitely a way to cash in, though, because wrestling at that time was still hot as balls, and Columbia got a top-five gold album out of it, so it all worked out for everyone.

My bosses at Columbia knew that I had a good relationship with Sharon Osbourne. She and I used to go out to the St. Regis Hotel and drink and tell stories while Ozzy would be upstairs sleeping. You could never get away with anything with her, trust me. After taking care of Ozzy all those years, she was wise to bullshit. One night at the St. Regis I snuck off to do some lines of blow in the lobby bathroom, and when I got back, she took one look at me and said, "Matt, you naughty boy." I mean, I thought I was acting pretty normal for me, but in one second, she nailed me. Ozzy was signed to the Epic side of Sony, but Epic was up to its ears in Osbourne-related projects: they had the family album from the television show, and an Ozzy live at Budokan album, and Kelly was making a record. They were Osbourned to the hilt. So Will and Donnie asked if I'd want to A&R an album recorded live at Ozzfest. I said, why not? I was friendly with all the bands on the bill, and I loved Sharon and Ozzy. It would be an easy one. Sharon and I had all these ideas about how to make it a special live album, because people just weren't buying live albums that much anymore. Sharon and I wanted to mix it up, do some unique duets and covers. We brought Thom Panunzio, who was an excellent producer and mixer as well as a friend and neighbor of Ozzy's, on board. I was looking forward to recording the festival and assembling the album.

Right around then, Sharon was diagnosed with breast cancer. She said, "Matt, I'm not going to be involved in making the record, but you have my blessings for anything you want to do." Without Sharon, *life with Ozzy* was a whole other ordeal. To be fair, he was beside himself, thinking that Sharon could die, and all these managers began to change their tune about getting involved, about doing duets and covers. It suddenly became too much work for them. There was no way, under these conditions, that I could rally people. I didn't intimidate them the way Sharon did, and with Ozzy checked out mentally, even more than usual, the bands only wanted to go out there, do their normal sets, collect their checks, and split. I did convince Drowning Pool's manager to have the band do Metallica's "Creeping Death," and they did a terrific version of it; the next week, their lead singer died on their tour bus. Someone at Columbia had the brilliant idea of releasing that track as the single from the album, which was just in the poorest taste imaginable.

I'd have pulled it off the album if it had been my decision. Another hitch was that we couldn't tell Ozzy the show was being recorded; we were afraid he'd flip out and freeze up if he knew, on top of everything else, that he had to nail the performance for an album. And his vocals would only be in top form early in the set.

All this was going on, and I'd scheduled a vacation with my wife and daughter, thinking the whole album would go smoothly and be wrapped up. The whole time we were away, I was getting frantic e-mails and phone calls. Mixes were being passed all over the place, and wires were getting crossed about what was approved and what wasn't. I was getting word from Columbia that we had to master the album in forty-eight hours to make the release date. It was a nightmare.

I'm sure I'm the only A&R person who went from quality-controlling Mary-Kate and Ashley's recordings to working with the WWF and Ozzy Osbourne. I was definitely learning the ropes, as well as being flung against them, but if you're going to survive doing A&R at a label like Columbia, you have to bring in hit acts. I finally got mine, including a heavy prog-rock band from Nyack, New York.

Encounters:
Coheed and Cambria

All rock bands come with the weight and influence of everything that preceded them. I remember the first time I heard Coheed and Cambria. Sometimes a band bends, and blends, genres to create a sound that's instantly their own. I called them "heavy prog rock," and that's as good a snapshot as any, but it doesn't describe the level of invention and ambition. This is going to sound insane, but imagine if Blue Cheer and Yes were transported into the future and collaborated on a concept album, zigging and zagging from power riffs to complex improvisations. Most people would call them a progressive band, in the tradition of King Crimson and Genesis, but unlike those bands, Coheed, to me, had the immediacy of classic hard rock. It only took one listen for me to be hooked.

Somebody sent me a copy of their album *The Second Stage Turbine Blade.* One track's title caught my attention: "Devil in Jersey City." I don't want to totally trash the place—there are some posh areas—but the city was a hellhole back then, decrepit and corrupt. I know there is a devil in Jersey City. Plus the music really grabbed me. I could hear all these diverse elements clanging against each other. I went to their show at Bowery Ballroom and there were maybe fifty people there, but the band played at peak arena velocity. The truly great bands don't give a shit how many people are in the room; they perform balls-out.

Then I went to see them at an outdoor festival in Jersey called Skate and Surf (later on, it morphed into the three-day Great Bamboozle), and this time there were a lot of kids checking them out. Claudio Sanchez had a unique voice; some people might compare it to Geddy Lee's, from Rush, but it's isn't as helium-ish. It has a fuller tone. And he wrote these epic songs and was an exceptional guitar player. Through the years, Coheed went through a bunch of personnel changes, but Claudio was always at the center of the storm. It was his vision, and it clicked with me. I knew I wanted to work with them. After the Skate and Surf set, I introduced myself. I could see them growing into something huge: there hadn't been a band in a very long time that wanted to stretch out lyrically and stylistically like that. Rock fans wanted elements of fantasy and grandeur in their music, and Coheed could grab that slot.

I had the green light from Columbia to sign Coheed. Great, except there may have been ten other labels who were at least intrigued. The chase was on. I could have waited to see them the next time they were in the area to make my Big Columbia Pitch, but any A&R person can tell you that those shows, especially in New York or LA, become what is lovingly referred to as a clusterfuck. I wanted to get more time with them alone. I booked a trip to the UK. I hopped on the Virgin train to see Coheed and Cambria open for Thrice at the Brixton Academy in London. That was the plan. I didn't know that Virgin trains between Manchester and London were famous for their lack of punctuality, and by the time my friends and I got to the venue, Coheed's set was over. I went backstage to say hi, and they were happy to see me. Meanwhile, my bosses were pressuring me to close. MTV had already decided that they were going to support the band and bang the first video. In the end it came down to only two contenders: RCA and Columbia. The band, their management, and their lawyer all concluded that they wanted to sign with me, but on the condition that we up our offer by $35,000. We caved, and Claudio said, "Man, I watched you growing up, and it's great that now I'm working with you."

Early reviews of their album were enthusiastic. Critics really seemed to get that this was something different (the phrase "new prog" was used), and not long after the album was released in the third quarter of 2003—record companies don't measure the calendar in weeks or months, only in financial quarters—it went gold.

MTV was a big part of Coheed's success. They were doing a prime-time (eight p.m.) live concert series and agreed to give Coheed a half-hour slot. That's unimaginable now, and it's only one of many reasons rock bands have such a difficult time breaking through. The concert, in Orlando, Florida, was a big deal for the band, and when I needed some exclusive material for international release—territories outside the US always wanted extra songs to keep their markets from being flooded with American imports—I mixed some of the tracks from that show. The problem was that MTV technically owned the rights to that performance, so rather than go through the whole clearance procedure, I just changed the information and said that the tracks were recorded in Tampa. Sorry, MTV.

The guys in Coheed became family to me. In the back of my mind, I always remembered what the veteran A&R guy Jason Flom (STP, Skid Row, Matchbox 20, Kid Rock, Lorde . . .) said to me when I was going to Columbia: "Matt, no matter what band you've got, or how close you get to them, there'll come a time when they'll turn on you." I didn't want to believe that, but I figured he must know what he was talking about. Still, I wanted to be friends with the artists I worked with. I owe a lot to Coheed, and I'm sure they'd say the same about me. Before them, I was due for a promotion to VP of A&R, and Will took me aside and said, "Listen, I don't think you should be a vice president yet. You'll be under the magnifying glass and I don't want everybody looking at every move you make." I understood what he meant: there were people upstairs glued to the balance sheets. I needed a hit to make people go, "Oh! That's why this guy is getting bumped up." Will was watching out for me. And it was cool. It wasn't even about the title. I was happy to be making records. Coheed grew my profile at the label tremendously, earned me my stripes, and were there for me during a difficult patch.

Coheed made me reappreciate some of the things I had lost touch with. I was going through problems in my marriage and had planned a family trip to Disney World with Yvette and Maya to reconnect. The whole vacation was paid for, but my wife decided not to go. Luckily, Maya was too young to realize what was going on, that she'd been gypped out of a vacation. My work had put a strain on our marriage. The late nights out, the constant traveling. It's the opposite of a nine-to-five job; it's a professional life that rolls into a social life and involves bars, clubs, parties, backstage, drugs, women, or at least the availability of women. People want to get you high and get you laid, and it's a hard life for a partner to adapt to. Unless you're really secure and well-adjusted, it can become "Where were you? Who were you with? Was [fill in the blank with the name of a hot girl your wife knows you work with and is already suspicious of] there?"

I was distraught about the vacation not happening, and I was on a call with Claudio and the band's manager, Blaze James, moaning about how all my plans had been blown out of the water. "You know what, man?" Blaze said. "We're going to Europe. There are twelve bunks on the bus, and one's empty. Fly yourself over and just go on the road with us."

Coheed were going to play some of the biggest festivals—Reading, Leeds—and the biggest cities, and I'd be along for the ride. I booked a flight to London and met the band at the famous Columbia Hotel, where every band stays when they're starting out. Oasis even wrote a song about it, "Columbia" ("There we were, now here we are"). After a long night of drinking, we got on the bus to the Reading Festival. From there, the tour went on to Leeds and then through the Continent. To get to the next stop, Peer, Belgium, the tour bus had to get on a ferry, but you couldn't stay in the vehicle. We were all fucking exhausted, drinking Jack and Cokes, watching a video jukebox. I was throwing on videos by the Jam and the Clash.

Somehow, we all fell asleep on the ferry, and when I woke up, everyone else was dead to the world. This is a small city in Belgium, I'd never been there before or even heard of it, but I decided to stroll around on my own. I needed some breakfast, and I found this little place to eat, and felt like I was in another world—which I was—until I heard the Beat playing on the radio, "Hands Off, She's Mine," and suddenly I felt in touch, like, Okay, I can hang here. As lost as I felt, my marriage crumbling, I heard this song and I felt good. The band had a packed house that night, and after the gig we explored Peer some more and found this whole alleyway with all these vending machines, dispensing everything from normal stuff, like sodas and candy bars, to underwear and wine.

Rock tours seem glamorous, but not so much when there

are about twenty guys traveling together who haven't showered. It gets kind of nutty, like when we all decided on the bus to Germany that it was going to be Freedom Night, where we all took off our shirts, played air guitar, and sang Led Zeppelin songs at the top of our lungs. This was just the release I needed, listening to classic rock music through the turns of the Swiss Alps. It was cinematic and panoramic and I thought, Shit, I'm sad I'm not at Disney World with my wife and kid, but this is an experience I'll probably never have again. It's definitely a younger man's game. To be with a band that's on the verge, to see the crowds responding, to know that everything is in front of them and that, at least in part, you're helping to make all that happen, that's one of the best feelings you can have in the world of rock. My last stop on the tour was in Bologna, where my friends Velvet Revolver were headlining. I'll always be grateful to the guys in Coheed for giving me that gift of distraction from what was going on back at home.

Coheed's follow-up album was tersely titled *Good Apollo, I'm Burning Star IV, Volume One: From Fear through the Eyes of Madness*. I've never written that out before, and never will again. It came out in 2005, hit *Billboard*'s top ten, and sold over a million copies worldwide. It received a rare perfect "100" score from the critic in *Alternative Press*, and *Q* magazine said it was "insane, but in a good way." What higher praise could you ask for? *Good Apollo,* I have to say, is the album I'm proudest of as an A&R guy.

Columbia treated Coheed with a lot of respect, but I still had to fight some fights. In the middle of the whole DualDisc fiasco, albums had to be a certain length to fit the extra video content, and *Good Apollo* was clocking in at around seventy-two minutes. "Matt," some executive I won't identify said to me, "can you talk the band into cutting a few songs to make the album closer to sixty minutes so that we can do a DualDisc?" I said, "This is an artist's art. It's a concept album. That's like asking the Who to take 'I'm Free' and 'Sensation' off *Tommy*. I can't do that." I told them I wouldn't even ask the band. I won that battle, but I had to cave and ask the band to add an extra chorus to the second single, "The Suffering," because the hook didn't hit until after the second verse. Shit like that is common practice at record labels, second-guessing and tinkering. There was such paranoia about albums leaking, how to get advance music out for press and promotion without the album ending up on the internet. The answer was: you couldn't. There's nothing you can do; it gets out, it gets downloaded. Everything taken into account, Coheed and Cambria was a peak A&R experience.

Pursuing the Killers
(and Other Adventures in A&R)

To do A&R means to lose a lot of the time. If you see an A&R guy played in a movie or television show, he's usually a predatory sleazebag in the backseat of a limo doing lines of coke off a stripper's fake tits. Okay, that part is true sometimes. But *most* of the time, it's a job of bad demos and showcases, the pressure to sign acts that pay the bills for that private sushi room, acts you sign that get lost in the system, acts you pass on that win Grammys. I think I got the hang of it at Columbia. We had a good A&R team with a strong track record. The swagger that came down from the top signaled a desire to win and, at least until Mottola left, the confidence that the hierarchy at the labels knew and cared about music. For the most part, the executives were on our side and gave us room to fail. They knew their stuff.

It was Don Ienner, in fact, who turned me on to a band that did really well for me. Someone at PromoSquad sent me a demo by a band called Sugardaddy Superstar, and the name was probably why I hadn't paid attention to it until I got a call from Ienner. He asked me to come up to his office to listen to it and played me the track "Cold." He wanted my take on it, and I told him I thought it could be a hit with different production, or at least a new mix. "Do you want to work on it?" "Yeah, of course." The label flew the band up from South Carolina for a showcase, and they did a nice job, but the first thing Donnie said to me was, "The name has got to go." Then he pivoted to the band and said, "I have four words for you: Toad the Wet Sprocket," basically telling them that no one would take "Sugardaddy Superstar" seriously. I worked with them on their album, picking apart what they'd already cut, poking through demos to find things that might have potential, finding a mixer to do polishing, rearranging songs, doing edits and remixes. I also gave them a list of possible band names to replace the crappy one they had, and they decided on Crossfade.

You're always saying to an artist, "Can you try this? I have this idea that might work. Indulge me for a half hour in the studio and let's see if it makes any difference. If you hate it, we'll erase it." Because no band wants to think they're being manipulated by the Label Guy. It's diplomacy. The head of Promotion might say, "Can you take out that part where the lead singer is screaming? Because it'll help get the record played more frequently in more day parts." And then you have to bring that to the band, and they might push back. So it becomes, "Hey, it's just a suggestion," but really you're pulling them toward where you want to take the mix or the edit or whatever you're doing. Other times, the promo guy would ask for something and I'd say, "I would never ask the artist to do something like that. So just live with it." On "Cold," we had to raise the vocal, get a better mix, and once it was right, it became a huge Active and Alternative Rock hit practically everywhere, except in New York and LA. It was a middle-America hit, No. 1 at the Active Rock format, and the only thing that kept the record from going to No. 1 at Alternative Rock was Green Day's "Boulevard of Broken Dreams." You couldn't fucking touch that record.

You couldn't dislodge it from No. 1 with a blowtorch. Two more Crossfade tracks, "So Far Away" and "Colors," were big airplay hits, and the album went platinum, selling close to two million copies.

I was aware of the band Midtown; they were part of the whole emo scene, came from my neck of the woods in Jersey—a few of them met at Rutgers—and were signed to Drive-Thru Records, a very influential label at that time, with bands like Dashboard Confessional, New Found Glory, Something Corporate. The label was the brainchild of a brother and sister, Richard and Stefanie Reines, who I knew when they were teenagers in New Brunswick. I used to see them at my friend's record store when they were like thirteen, fourteen; they'd done their hair like Mike Peters, the lead singer of the band the Alarm. They decided to start their own label, and it turned into this huge company. Midtown was signed to their label, but they felt they were getting secondary treatment from Drive-Thru, especially after Richard and Stefanie made a distribution deal with MCA. One night, my assistant, Allison, and I were walking uptown from a showcase at Mercury Lounge and wound up near Irving Plaza, and all of a sudden we bumped into Gabe, Midtown's lead singer. "Hey, we're playing tonight. Come in and see us." They were the opening band, and Allison and I went upstairs to watch. They were playing a batch of new material and I looked at Allison, who is so savvy and so clued-in, and said, "We've got to get these guys." It was just so strong. The next day, Gabe came up to my office with a CD that was basically recorded on one mic in the middle of a rehearsal room. But I was sold. I got my friend Jonathan Daniel from Crush Management into it, and he suggested Butch Walker to produce some real demos. I got the okay to spend some Columbia demo money, but the wheels of a record label grind slowly, and by the time the funds were cleared, the band and Butch had gone ahead and done the demos on their own, self-financed.

Here's where the wheels started to fall off. I'd brought in Jonathan, and Butch had cut the tracks pro bono, but we had no deal. We hadn't made any investment, there was nothing on paper. The demos started getting around, a lawyer was shopping the band, and it became a hyper-competitive situation. I mean, I had competition from Epic, which was right in our own building, under the Sony roof. Don Ienner was running the whole Sony operation, and he was trying to help steer Midtown to Epic. Will went ballistic: "This would not even exist without Matt!" Other labels like Atlantic and DreamWorks wanted them, and I was freaking out, because if I hadn't bumped into Gabe on Irving Place that night and gotten this started, this bidding war wouldn't be happening. Finally, we won out at Columbia. There was some residual fallout from the Epic battle, though. Midtown was booked to open for another Sony band, on Epic, called Lostprophets; they didn't get a sound check, and Gabe was off his game because he couldn't hear his vocals. Of course, Ienner was in the room, and he was already ticked off about the band choosing Columbia over Epic, so all he needed was a so-so Midtown performance to decide, as Sony's chairman, that he wasn't going to seriously back the band anymore.

There's no logic to any of this. Crossfade was basically something that walked in the door, sounded like there might be a hit on it, and wound up going through the roof. Midtown was fought for and labored over and was basically declared dead on arrival. It's the nature of the game, and you can't relitigate. In retrospect, there was only one act I feel as though I shed blood for and lost, a group that went on to fulfill all the potential I heard the moment someone played me their demo.

Get any A&R person drunk, and when it's late enough, he or she will tell you the story of the one that got away, the one heartbreaking musical pursuit. Everyone has one of those, and it doesn't matter how many platinum albums you have hanging on your office wall. To trace mine back to the start, we have to return to the England trip where I saw Coheed. I was on the train with Alex Gilbert, the UK A&R exec at Warner Bros. He played me some songs by a band from Las Vegas, the Killers. I'm not sure how a UK guy got his hands on that demo, or why I hadn't. But holy shit: "On Top," "Smile Like You Mean It," "Who Let You Go," and "Mr. Brightside." Four great songs on one demo. Gilbert had already played the songs for a friend at the UK indie Lizard King Records. I knew I had to track them down (that took a while, because they were still very much under the radar). First I made a quick trip to Colorado City, where I met with some musicians who were returning from active duty in Iraq. I judged a battle-of-the-bands contest and entertained the troops in my way, which I can tell you was a lot different from Bob Hope bringing Ann-Margret to boost the spirits—among other things—of GIs during the Vietnam War. Despite my lack of comedic chops, and not having any eye candy in my entourage (or having an entourage at all), I was warmly greeted by the troops. Many of them remembered seeing me on MTV. After all they'd been through, they wanted me to tell them stories about their favorite bands. I guess I represented someone who was familiar, someone who was living a kind of fantasy life. I was a bridge between worlds.

From Colorado, I hopped on a flight to Vegas to meet the Killers, and was driven to drummer Ronnie Vannucci's parents' house. They were rehearsing in a dimly lit garage. Blankets covered the walls as soundproofing. Dave Grohl says everybody sucks at the beginning; that's the beauty of what you do as a band—you stumble around and you basically suck until you don't. Nothing comes out of the gate perfectly, and the Killers had the same arc—one major booking agent I know saw them early on and passed—but hell, I was knocked out. That happens less often than you might imagine, when you're in the room and you just know like that; it all unfolds right in front of you. Even in a garage.

For dinner we went to a steakhouse and were joined by a couple of Columbia's West Coast A&R guys. Even inside a label, people can get a little competitive. They want to put their mark on something early. At dinner, Brandon Flowers, the band's singer and songwriter, and the rest of the guys kept asking me to tell them about Bowie, tell them about the Cure or the Psychedelic Furs. They were so young and naïve. Brandon was still a bellboy at a Vegas hotel. One of the other band members was working at, like, a urine-testing place for pro athletes; another was earning his money at a quickie-wedding joint. That's how bizarre this game is: they're just another local band with a demo, all of them with day jobs, and at the same time they're being bought steak dinners on a Sony expense account. And other labels were giving them a serious look. That's another thing about the business: there are no secrets, and bidding wars can start as quickly as California brushfires. How do any of these kids keep their equilibrium? One night they're fans, drinking record company booze and rattling off questions about Bowie, and within days they could be signed to the same record company that released Bowie's most recent album. It can give a band whiplash.

Later on that night, it was just me and Brandon in his car, a blue AMC. The car didn't even have a CD player, only a cassette player and two cassettes: the Beatles' *1962–1966* (aka *The Red Album*) and the Beatles' *Help!* I picked *Help!*, and for the next ten minutes or so, Brandon and I zipped down the Strip singing the album's first three songs at the top of our lungs: "Help!," "The Night Before," and "You've Got to Hide Your Love Away." I looked at Brandon and I could see how jazzed he was that we were having this moment. The Beatles were, still are, the ultimate musical unifier. We went into the lounge for more drinks, and I told him more rock tales. We talked about my hanging with the Iraq vets, and got into much deeper stuff. Life stuff, goals, relationships, fears. It was a weird period in my life, and I was just being honest with him. Maybe I had too much to drink—it's been known to happen. I am that guy; that's my double-edged sword. It's who I am. I have no filter for emotion. There we were at the bar, Brandon was picking my brain and telling me his own story about growing up Mormon in Salt Lake City.

Flash-forward to when their album came out in June 2004. I was drawn to a track, track five, "All These Things That I've Done." It was one of the high points of *Hot Fuss* and was nominated for a Grammy. Braden Merrick, the band's manager at the time, told me that right after the talk Brandon and I had had that night in Vegas, Brandon went home and wrote the song. The line "I got soul but I'm not a soldier" was inspired by my story about the vets.

"You've got to hear the song Brandon wrote about you," Braden had said to me on the phone when I was still in the running to sign the band. Now, Brandon might not want to say that out loud, and maybe he'd say it's more personal, or a composite or whatever, but every time I hear the song I think about the night in Vegas. The song is an anguished cry, in the voice of someone who doesn't want to be put "on the back burner." We're all getting older and getting on and have anxiety about what's next, and that's what this song captures so intensely. My ex-girlfriend said to me, "You know, this song is not one hundred percent complimentary," and maybe that's the case, but it's about a guy going through a crisis in his life, and to the extent that Brandon might have drawn on our night for its inspiration, that's what he picked up on.

I played those Killers demos for everyone at the label, from the chairman to the assistants, and they were all on board. It came down to Columbia and Island Def Jam, the final two labels in contention, and I thought we had a solid shot at getting them, never underestimating the competition. Island's Rob Stevenson was a sharp A&R guy, and the company's boss, Lyor Cohen, is a ruthless *macher* who cut his teeth in the world of hip-hop and relishes a battle. Lyor and Donnie battling it out was something you'd want a ringside seat for. The heat was on, and I had one card to play: I was on the air at K-Rock, and since the Killers were an unsigned band, there'd be no conflict of interest if I brought them on the air. When the band came to New York City for the decision-making meetings, the only time I got them to myself was on a Sunday afternoon, and they came up to the station to play their songs acoustically for me to air on my weekly show, the Buzz. I gave "Mr. Brightside" and other Killers tunes exposure on the biggest alternative rock station in the country. Top that, IDJ!

Now all they had to do was meet with Donnie and Will, have them do their "Columbia is the number-one record company in the world and you'll be joining the most prestigious artist roster" spiel, and that would be that. Done deal. But Lyor and Island were breathing down the band's neck (literally, knowing Lyor), and I had to get them in the room with my bosses to close. The problem was that there was a big charity dinner that Donnie and Will had to go to; Beyoncé and John Mayer, two of the hottest artists on the label, were going to be there. Will said I should bring the band up to 550 Madison the next day. That was all the time Lyor needed to basically say, What do we need to do to close this out now? He was ready to give them whatever they wanted on the spot, and since he was the top cat, he could deliver. I was just an A&R guy. Finally, Will said to bring them up to the building on Friday morning. On Thursday, the night before our scheduled meeting, Island got the band a limo, had all the paperwork done, the whole contract. Later, Braden told me, "Matt, the band loves you, but when the guy who signs the checks says, 'What do I have to do to be in the Killers business?,' it's really hard to turn that down." Lyor pulled out all the stops; he was not going to lose this band to Columbia.

In the end, Lyor and Rob signed the Killers. Brandon came over to the Sony building to tell me the news. "Matt, listen, we love you, but Lyor and those guys, they're just so passionate about it." I didn't get super upset; I told him I loved his music and wished the band the best. Debut album, triple platinum in the US, five Grammy nominations. You can't hate people for the business decisions they make. It was a tough loss, but I also realized that this kind of thing happens to everyone. I congratulated them on getting their record deal, and they took me out to dinner with some of their new Island Def Jam money. What I didn't understand were the people at Sony telling me not to stay friendly with the band because they fucked me over. First of all, they didn't fuck me over; they had a choice between two excellent record companies and picked the one that seemed to want them more. Second, if I like this band enough to want to sign them and mentor them and be an integral part of their career, am I supposed to cut them loose and tell them to screw off for the rest of their lives because they didn't sign with me? As it turned out, my relationship with the Killers outlasted my relationship with Columbia. I've spent so much time with them over the years. When they did their Live 8 appearance, I covered it for MTV.

Before the show, Braden caught up with me and said, "They're going to do your song tonight." They invited me up to the side of the stage, and I looked out at the crowd of 175,000 watching the Killers and the choir do "All These Things That I've Done" and thought about my ride with Brandon that started this whole thing. The Killers were now one of the biggest bands in the world, playing this huge rock event. That's how quickly they made the leap from the blanket-padded garage.

My record company life ended abruptly. I got a call from Don Ienner's assistant telling me to come up to his office. He dropped the news on me that I was being let go in a round of layoffs. I was one of only two people at the label that he was telling in person. The rest were going to be fired by an HR person. That was that. I guess I should have been devastated, but after the shock wore off, I realized that this was the nature of the ride: it would give you thrills, moments of elation, and then it would be over. It was an incredible experience for me to get to work at a label with such history. I had the chance to help create records that are still in the Columbia catalog. I caught the very last wave, I think, of real artist development, being able to take a chance on any number of new things. In the early 2000s, hit albums were really Hit Albums that sold millions of copies, so there was all this money trickling down (thanks, Beyoncé; thanks, Savage Garden; thanks, John Mayer and Train) to support new signings and keep A&R departments humming.

You would walk down the hall on the twenty-fourth floor of the Sony building and there were maybe a dozen A&R people blasting music from their offices, sharing music with each other, getting opinions and feedback, inviting each other to come along to showcases. We had our own little performance space on our floor where bands could come and play for us. I felt like part of a team, bearing witness to all this creativity. I met people like Don DeVito, an A&R guy who'd been with Columbia since the 1960s, had worked with artists like Bob Dylan, the Byrds, Janis Joplin, and James Taylor, had scandalous, hilarious stories about the most unlikely artists on the label (two words: moon river), and was the ultimate music business mensch who taught me so much. When I turned on CNN in November 2011 and saw that he'd passed away, I thought, Well, that's the last tie to the true history of Columbia. At least the history I knew. I feel so fortunate that our paths crossed when they did. And that I was part of the tail end of when the record industry was still a wild adventure.

I guess it's easiest to blame the decline of the business

on file sharing (which my bosses called "stealing"), but any music fan could have looked at Napster and known that there was no reversing the path of that storm. I loved the idea of everything being at my actual fingertips. You mean I can think of a song I want to hear and have it in seconds for free? If I were a kid, or in college, I would have done exactly the same thing all the people on Napster were doing. A friend of mine said, "Hell, if I could have turned on my radio when I was thirteen years old and pressed a button to keep the songs and play them whenever I wanted, I'd have pressed the fucking button." Who wouldn't? I still would have bought records, because I'd want to know all the details and credits you couldn't get on a downloaded Napster track, but the existence of the "keep this" button was a revolution, and no one in the business, at least no one on the executive floors at Sony, knew what to do about it. Once in a while, in a label meeting, someone younger and hipper, like Mark Ghuneim, who eventually became the label's Senior Vice President of Online and Emerging Technologies, would try to explain, patiently, why certain antitheft strategies were impractical, but the company was still trying to figure out how to deactivate that button and get people to buy more CDs. We all can see how well that turned out.

On an emotional level, I was torn, and I defended bands like Metallica who took a stand. Why should somebody who paints your house or serves you a Happy Meal get paid, and someone who makes a song you love be expected to give their work away? I get it. I was sympathetic. But it was a game of Whac-a-Mole: shut down LimeWire and something else will pop up.

Now it was time for something new.

50 ESSENTIAL ROCK ALBUMS:
THE '00s

Acceptance—*Phantoms*

Ryan Adams—*Heartbreaker*

Arcade Fire—*Funeral*

Animal Collective—*Merriweather Post Pavilion*

Arctic Monkeys—*Whatever People Say I Am, That's What I'm Not*

Audioslave

Biffy Clyro—*Puzzle*

The Black Keys—*Attack & Release*

David Bowie—*Heathen*

Cage the Elephant

Coheed and Cambria—*Good Apollo, I'm Burning Star IV, Volume One: From Fear through the Eyes of Madness*

Coldplay—*A Rush of Blood to the Head*

Death Cab for Cutie—*Transatlanticism*

Deftones—*White Pony*

Editors—*An End Has a Start*

Eminem—*The Marshall Mathers LP*

Foo Fighters—*Wasting Light*

The Gaslight Anthem—*The '59 Sound*

Gorillaz—*Demon Days*

Green Day—*American Idiot*

Incubus—*Morning View*

Interpol—*Turn on the Bright Lights*

Keane—*Hopes and Fears*

The Killers—*Hot Fuss*

Kings of Leon—*Only by the Night*

Linkin Park—*Hybrid Theory*

Midtown—*Forget What You Know*

Mumford & Sons—*Sigh No More*

Muse—*Black Holes and Revelations*

My Chemical Romance—*The Black Parade*

My Morning Jacket—*Z*

Nine Inch Nails—*With Teeth*

Outkast—*Speakerboxxx/The Love Below*

A Perfect Circle—*Mer de Noms*

Phoenix—*Alphabetical*

Queens of the Stone Age—*Songs for the Deaf*

The Raconteurs—*Consolers of the Lonely*

Radiohead—*Kid A*

The Roots—*Phrenology*

The Shins—*Chutes Too Narrow*

Spoon—*Ga Ga Ga Ga Ga*

The Strokes—*Is This It*

System of a Down—*Toxicity*

Tool—*Lateralus*

U2—*All That You Can't Leave Behind*

Vampire Weekend

The White Stripes—*Elephant*

Wilco—*Yankee Hotel Foxtrot*

Amy Winehouse—*Back to Black*

Encounters:
Bowie

New York City, 2002

I'm standing by the mixing board at the Hit Factory, and my cellphone rings.

"Hey, Matt. It's David Bowie."

What the fuck? David Bowie is calling me?

"I'd love to have you over to my place on Wednesday and play my album for you, get your opinion on some people you think might be good remixers, or some marketing ideas."

Okay. My life is officially weird.

At this point, I was doing A&R for Columbia Records, and every week we had an executive luncheon, so I said to David Bowie, "Yeah, that would be amazing. Wednesday I have the label meeting, so how's Thursday or Friday?"

To this day, I laugh at myself. I mean, what if Wednesday was the only day he could meet me? What kind of ridiculous thing is that to say? I immediately felt like a complete idiot.

"I'll tell you what, Matt, Thursday or Friday I'll send you an e-mail with the address, and you can come over."

So I went to his apartment. We sat on opposite couches. His assistant, Coco, was the only other person in the room. She was in the corner taking notes on the things I was saying about each song. And Bowie was listening intently, and all I could think was, David Bowie is listening to me, asking for my input on his music, considering my suggestions for what songs should go on his next album.

We listened to the entire *Heathen* album in its original form, and then Coco said to me, "You know, David has five other songs that I really wish he'd play for you. Come on, David."

"Ah, I don't know. I'm not sure how I feel about them, or if I really think they're finished . . ."

And all of a sudden—you know me, fearless—I blurted out, "David, you've got to play them for me! Let's hear 'em!" He finally agreed, reluctantly.

He played me the first song, a cover of Neil Young's "I've Been Waiting for You."

I jumped up. "David, you have to put this on the album!"

He was a little taken aback. Not that he didn't agree with me, but that I was so emphatic. Then he played "Slow Burn," which he was not going to include on the album, and as we listened, I could see that he was starting to second-guess himself. He's pacing back and forth. There's a terrace, with a little garden, and he's walking in and out smoking cigarettes, and then he looks at me.

"So what do you think of this one?"

"It's fucking great. It has to be on the album." (It was, and a year later earned Bowie a Grammy nomination.)

Then a third song, another "outtake," "Everybody Says Hi," another song I said should go on. "I don't know what to tell you, David. These songs are amazing," It's the funniest thing in the world. Each song he'd discarded, I'm saying he was wrong. There's a fourth song, and this time he looks at me with a challenging look.

"All right. What about this one?"

"Ah, B-side. Or a song for a soundtrack."

He took two fingers, wiped them on his brow like, "Whew." Like, "Thank God, at least I called this one correctly."

"You know, that's one of the things I love about you, Matt, that you really know so much and are so passionate about music, and you know things that even I've forgotten about the music I've done."

"Well, David," I finally said, "you're responsible for that. You are more responsible for that than you'll ever know."

For my thirteenth birthday, in 1974, I got the *Diamond Dogs* album. I was just hitting puberty. Thinking about fucking, obviously, just being with a girl. I remember hearing the line "Hot tramp, I love you so," and thinking how sexual that was, how flippant. "Holy shit," I thought. "How badass." It's like why young kids get into hip-hop today, because there's an air of danger in it.

It's been well documented that there was a lot of alcohol, a lot of cocaine at the time, and straight through to the *Young Americans* and *Station to Station* sessions. In the 1975 Bowie documentary *Cracked Actor*, you can see how wired-up he is. He looks so thin and frail. At the time, I didn't even know what cocaine was. I just thought Bowie was dark and cool.

The truth is, I got completely immersed in *Diamond Dogs*. It made me look further and deeper. Because of my older brother, Glenn, and my sister-in-law, I already had the third Velvet Underground album, and I would listen to "What Goes On" and "Beginning to See the Light," so I already had a glimpse of that undercurrent, but then Bowie came along.

I asked a friend, "Hey, man, have you heard David Bowie's 'Rebel Rebel'?"

"No, have you heard 'Space Oddity'?"

"What the fuck is that?"

When the single came out originally, it was a hit in England, but not in the US. Many people saw it as a novelty record, like a one-hit-wonder thing.

"What is it? Let me hear it."

I remember how wild the song was, that the space guy dies and goes off into outer space. It was scary. It was intense. *Ziggy Stardust* was the next Bowie record I got. I liked the idea of Ziggy Stardust; he echoed my childhood dreams. I wanted to be a musician, I wanted to be a rock star, and the lyrics were about this guy finding his way through that, plus there were so many sexual overtones that for a twelve-year-old kid with blow jobs on the brain, it was magnetic.

I heard my friends were starting a band, and I went to the basement where they rehearsed. They had another guy singing and he wasn't very good. I said, "Hey, guys, why don't I try to do it?" I got up there and asked if they did "Rebel Rebel," and, sure enough, they went, "You're our singer now." The other kid became the manager. The band was called Thunderhead. I know that's a terrible name, and it sounds like a metal band, but hell, we were thirteen, fourteen years old. We learned "Walk This Way" by Aerosmith, "All Right Now" by Free, "Can't Get Enough of Your Love" by Bad Company, and of course we kept "Rebel Rebel" in our sets, along with two or three other Bowie songs. The next thing you know, we were playing the teen center in East Brunswick, and junior high dances. We were the kings! Each of us earned about thirty-five dollars.

When I was about fourteen and had my aneurysm, long hair was very much still in play, and with my bald, scarred skull, I looked alien and felt alienated. That summer Bowie's movie *The Man Who Fell to Earth* came out, and maybe to make me feel better, I went with some of my friends to see it. The mom of Thunderhead's guitar player brought me *Aladdin Sane* when I was still in the hospital, so as soon as I got home I started listening to that, and to *Hunky Dory*. Bowie was always kind of there, a touchstone for a scattered army of misfit kids.

Remember, back then there was no internet, so a fan really had to dig. I would drive forty-five minutes to find a guy who had Bowie's English singles and pay him ten bucks for an import 45, to get the songs I didn't have. To get his cover of the Jacques Brel song "Amsterdam" on the B-side of "Sorrow," or the alternate—not the disco version, but the cool Mick Ronson one that's all fucked-up sounding and goes nuts at the end—"John, I'm Only Dancing," you would have to hunt for someone who sold it. When I was older, I realized that at Bleecker Bob's and Golden Discs they had all those records, but it was an adventure to get in a car, meet someone, and pay for the singles, like a drug deal.

I was fifteen when I got to see Bowie in person. I was seeing a girl named Lisa (I thought I was going to lose my virginity to her, but that didn't happen), and her older sister was going out with Johnny Thunders from the New York Dolls. The four of us went to Nassau Coliseum on Long Island on March 23, 1976, for a concert on what was officially called the Isolar tour, but which most people just call the Station to Station tour, or the Thin White Duke tour. I thought I knew what to expect, because I'd been spending so much time listening to every Bowie LP and had delved so deeply into the *David Live* album that marked a turning point between the eras of *Diamond Dogs* and *Young Americans* and introduced me to Bowie songs I hadn't been aware of before. But I learned quickly that you never can anticipate what a Bowie show is going to be like. For starters, before Bowie even came onstage, the audience watched the 1929 short film *Un Chien Andalou* by Luis Buñuel and Salvador Dalí, known mostly for the shocking image of an eyeball being sliced by a razor blade, a shot so graphic that the crowd, every night, let out a collective scream. (Years later, Bowie told me, "The second I heard that scream, I knew I had exactly ten minutes to get onstage.") Then the show itself started with a long version of "Station to Station," with the line "This is the stuff from which dreams are woven," and that's how I felt: this *was* a dream made real, and I remember the whole concert in black-and-white, vivid and stark, David looking skeletal in his crisp white shirt and dark vest, his hair slicked back, the stage unadorned. This tour wasn't about spectacle, it was about the songs. Nothing was embellished; the theatrics were stripped away, and what remained was pure artistry. The show ended with three of my favorite songs ever, "Diamond Dogs," "The Jean Genie," and "Rebel Rebel," and I left the arena in a daze.

As I discovered new artists, and they would come and go, my love for Bowie never stopped. I watched him do "Boys Keep Swinging" on *SNL*. My high school girlfriend and I got tickets to see him on Broadway in *The Elephant Man*. Sat in the second row. When the whole new wave thing happened, the post-punk thing, all of those artists were into him. For all those UK bands like Echo and the Bunnymen, Ultravox, and Joy Division, *Ziggy Stardust* was a life-changing event, like in the '60s when all those kids were inspired to form bands by seeing the Beatles do "I Want to Hold Your Hand" on *The Ed Sullivan Show*. It was a catalyst for them, the Psychedelic Furs, Duran Duran, who covered "Fame." You can hear it in the synth bands.

When I was on the air at Rutgers and HTG, I kept playing every Bowie project, even though I have to admit he kind of lost me for a while after 1983's *Let's Dance*. I felt as though I had an obligation to let überfans like me know what he was up to, no matter what I personally thought of his albums with Tin

Machine, or *Black Tie White Noise*. As much as I didn't love the *Black Tie* album, it has a prominent place in my memory, because that's the first time I ever spoke to David. He phoned in to HTG so I could interview him about it, and while part of me thought, I got this, another part was looking in from the outside and saying, Are you joking? The way I saw it, it was a privilege to finally be able to talk to him, even about this project. My feelings about him went way beyond any specific album.

I didn't meet Bowie until 1995, two decades after his music turned my head inside out. Some MTV people were going to have dinner with him; Virgin Records rented out the entire back room at the Bowery Bar, a lot of tables, and everyone was saying, "The biggest Bowie fan at the station is Matt!" Someone told Bowie, "There's one guy in the music department who's a huge fan."

I walked up to him and said, "Hey, I'm Matt Pinfield. I've been in the music department for a few months, and I just need to let you know that you're one of my favorite artists of all time." It wasn't the most original opening line, but he was very nice to me, and we took a picture together, and I figured that was that. Then Michael Plen, a guy from Virgin, said, "Matt, you're going to sit opposite David." There were four dinner tables, and I was put right across from Bowie, with all the MTV network heads. I thought, "Fuck, this is either going to go great, or terribly fucking wrong." I asked the waitress to bring me a Jack and Coke.

I started asking him all of the things I'd always wanted to know about: Mick Ronson, how he picked certain covers for *Pin-Ups*, earlier versions of Ziggy songs, all this stuff, firing questions at him, rocking the Jack and Cokes. An MTV executive asked David's wife, Iman, if she knew as much about his music as I did. "I don't know if that's possible," she said.

Then he told me, "Matt, I'm going to tell you something no-body knows. I'm going to go on the road with Nine Inch Nails, we're going to headline a tour together, and I want to ask you a favor. I'd love to get your ideas for a set list. I'm going to give you my number. I want to know what songs I should do live that aren't singles, that the younger audience you're involved with would connect to."

Right there at the table, I started to give him a list of some of the Bowie songs the newer bands had been getting into: STP's "Andy Warhol," Nirvana's "The Man Who Sold the World," Smashing Pumpkins' "Moonage Daydream." Off the top of my head. He probably already knew about some of them, because he was aware of everything. After I rattled off some titles, I asked David if I could fax him a more extensive list the next day.

Later that night, I was too jacked up to go home, so I went down to the Golden Lion on Bleecker, ran into some old friends, and continued drinking. I probably would have lost Bowie's phone number, but Steven Hill from MTV was smart enough to hold on to the piece of paper for me until the next morning.

Through the years, with some long gaps, David would get in touch, mostly when he had a question he wanted to ask, or if he was curious about what I thought of a new band. We had one e-mail conversation when the debut album by Arcade Fire came out in 2004. "I'd love to know your opinion about this," he wrote. "I'm over the moon about them." He said that his favorite track on *Funeral* was "Neighborhood #3 (Power Out)," and I wrote back, "I love 'Wake Up.'" E-mail was the perfect means of communication for him, and I wish I'd saved those exchanges, because he was so engaged about new music, so erudite and charming, and I was beyond flattered that he wanted to know my take on music. It always seemed as though I'd been chosen, but I imagine he made many other people feel that way: he was genuinely curious, and although he was so private and circumspect, in social settings he had a gift for extracting information and opinion that he could use.

The last time I saw David, at the end of our conversation he pulled me aside and said, "I know you're friends with Scott Weiland. Please let him know that I'm here to talk if he needs someone." I think he spotted in Scott a kindred soul. Not only musically—you can hear the Bowie influence so powerfully on STP songs like "And So I Know" on their third album, and "Kitchenware & Candybars" on *Purple*—but in terms of the demons he was fighting. So backstage at one of his solo shows I passed along that offer to Scott, and he said, "I'd love to talk to him." That was my final encounter with Scott. By the start of 2016, both he and Bowie were gone.

I'd certainly heard that Bowie was in quite ill health, but nothing could have prepared me for the news I got early in the morning on January 10. On Sunday afternoon, I made a stop at Vintage Vinyl off Route 1 in Fords, New Jersey, to do something I'd been doing ritualistically for four decades, go to a record store—one of the last free-standing independent stores in Jersey—to buy a new David Bowie album as soon as it was released. There is something about the beauty of walking up to the counter and buying an album, I miss that, and I know I could have downloaded *Blackstar* instantly online, or streamed it, but that's not what my connection to Bowie's music was like. I had to physically buy it—I got the CD and the vinyl—and own it and take it home and absorb it the way I'd done with every Bowie album since I was a preteen.

The thing that's really hit me this year is that we all face our mortality, and one reason we fall in love with music is that, for a while, it makes us feel invincible. But it also reflects our shortcomings and our fears. We're all just trying to find our way, and we look for music to help guide us, for songs that make us think, "That's exactly where I am right now at this moment in my life." And that's because we can hear what the artist is grappling with and we can relate to it, and when I listened to *Blackstar* after finding out, at around three in the morning, that Bowie had passed away, I thought about how he elevated the Art of the Album and how, with his death, that Art has become lost. He took the medium to a level of self-invention (and re-invention) and self-discovery. You hear so many artists admit, "We're not making albums anymore." *Blackstar* doesn't only feel like a last statement from Bowie, a chapter in a sequence that goes back to *The Man Who Sold the World* and *Hunky Dory*, and on to *Ziggy* and *Aladdin Sane*, and *Low* and *Heroes*, and *Heathen* and *Reality*. He shaped each album in a very specific, conceptual, cinematic way, and he never stopped doing that. Every album had a consistent point of view, and he revealed himself through character or genre or narrative. I thought, There goes the last artist who cared about making the album more than a collection of songs.

He was my inspiration. He always knew, "I can't rest on this." He was always looking ahead. To the Next Thing. That's what I learned from him when I was a kid listening to his albums in my bedroom: you don't have to settle, or say, This is all there is. His vision was expansive and made geeky kids face the strange without fear.

To the end, Bowie kept his mystique, which is so hard in this day and age, with all the technology and the fact that today you know what every artist has had for breakfast. And he did that by trusting only a certain number of people. I'm telling the story about me and him, but it's really for the music fan reading this who wants to work with bands, to say that it can happen, that you can gain the respect of the artists that you love the most. The thirteen-year-old who auditioned for a band singing "Rebel Rebel" because it was revealing secrets about sex and mystery and was a jolt to the system—he could never have imagined it.

Coda:
Is Rock Dead?

Leslie Fram and me with Green Day

W hen I found myself exiled from the record industry,
along with quite a number of my friends, some of
whom had been in the game far longer than I had been, I
was lucky that I had a fallback position. I was able to continue presenting music on TV and radio. I'd been asked
by friends at VH1, Tom Calderone and Rick Krim, to host
the channel's *Top 20 Countdown*, and I had a good time
doing that. And I was approached by another new media
venture being started by Mark Cuban. He and a partner
started HDNet in 2001, and they were looking for more
original high-definition programming, so once again—as at
Farmclub—I was thrown into a place where the public was
lagging behind the technology.

Really, there wasn't much, as they say, market penetration

in the area of high-definition TV. An entire channel devoted to HD was pretty forward-thinking and radical. So was the idea of putting my face into people's homes in high definition. You sink a few grand into a new TV set that shows everything in startling clarity, every crevice and wrinkle, and there I am practically in three dimensions in your living room. I can't imagine what they were thinking. If I were to kick off an HD channel, it wouldn't be with Matt Pinfield and Dan Rather. Some faces are better viewed in low-def. But they brought me to host a show called *Sound Off with Matt Pinfield*, and it was me and two HD cameras, one trained on me, the other on my guest, doing one-on-one interviews. Again, for someone with an investment in HD, it may not have been visually impressive, but I got the biggest kick out of doing the show. They still run the pieces I did on AXS TV, and they're some of my favorite interviews ever, including with legends Les Paul and Tony Bennett.

I first met Les Paul with Metallica, after one of his weekly performances at the Iridium. When I interviewed him years later, he must've been around ninety years old but was still sharp as a tack. "Nice to see you again, Matt," he said, and it was mind-blowing to me that he even remembered who I was, or that we'd met before. He told me about coming home from Germany after World War II, and how he'd started experimenting with music on tape recorder. He would overlay sound on sound when no one was even thinking about things like overdubbing. He built his first guitar out of a piece of railroad lumber. That made me think of my dad, and how he would use every piece of equipment he could get his hands on to make me my first radio transmitter. He said that in the late '40s, Bing Crosby asked him to be in his band, and he said, "Bing, I'm sorry, I'm working on my own thing." He was just down in this basement, tinkering around, trying to fulfill his own ideas of what he wanted to do musically, and that wound up changing everything. I was fascinated by him, by his brilliance, energy, and humor.

I think what I've been able to do is beyond what someone on the *Today* show or *Good Morning America* does. A musician goes on those shows and the host is reading questions off note cards prepared by some junior researcher. The way I see it, there's the überfan on one side of the spectrum, wanting to know every tiny detail, and then there's the person who's a casual listener and doesn't care about the minutiae, and it's my job to be in the middle of that spectrum. I'm translating for the super-informed fanatic and the person who's more of a blank slate.

Between HDNet and VH1 and being on the radio on WRXP—I was hosting the morning-drive shift with Leslie Fram—I was busier than ever, and even had to turn down a job at Atlantic Records. Lyor Cohen, the executive who grabbed the Killers out of Columbia's clutches, offered me a job on the condition that I be exclusive to them and not do all the other TV and radio gigs, and I couldn't do that. I felt that not only was I doing what I was meant to do, but I was having more fun than ever doing it. Leslie and I were running wild at RXP, doing things like renting a double-decker bus as a promotion for UK band the Kooks and taking people on a New York City Rock Tour. The band was on the bus playing their acoustic guitars, and I was showing the listeners all the famous musical sites of the city. We learned firsthand why the regular Big Apple Tour buses stick to the wider avenues. As we went east on St. Mark's Place, I pointed out the club where the Velvet Underground played their first gig in the city, the building that's on the cover of Led Zep's *Physical*

Graffiti, the stoop where Mick and Keith sat in the "Waiting on a Friend" video, and then I turned around and I saw that we were about to get clipped by a combination of telephone wires and tree branches. All I could see were the lawsuits. I yelled out, "Everybody duck!" and we hit the ground.

I got to hang out with Tony Bennett at his recording studio in New Jersey. The studio was a converted train station, so when he did his vocals, a natural echo bounced off the walls. Bennett confided in me that, back in the '70s, he'd had his own problems with drugs. Seeing how vibrant and vital he was after going through a period of excess, that struck a chord with me. My own battles with substance abuse have certainly been no secret. I bounced in and out of rehab quite a few times over the years, trying to get a handle on my dependency. It didn't stick. Drugs were everywhere. If you're even the slightest bit tempted, being in the rock game is no way to abstain, but the rock game was the only one I knew, and I had to figure out a way to stay alive and stay sober.

It was trial after trial, from church basements in New York City to the Caron Foundation facility in Pennsylvania, where members of Aerosmith got clean (and built the gym), to Las Encinas with Dr. Drew. I wanted to kick my addiction, and as anyone who's been in and out of rehab will tell you, it's no fucking cakewalk. In 2009 it clobbered me again, and I knew I needed help. I had to have a talk with the station's general manager, because I was losing it. She said, "Matt, we know you want to go away and deal with this, and we need you to go away. There are two ways you can handle it: you can either not tell your audience and disappear for twenty-eight days, and everyone will speculate, or you can go on the air and talk about it. It's your choice." She told me my job would be there when I got out. I could've made something up, I suppose, told our listeners that I was off to do some secret movie project or going on a tour, but I decided to deal with it on the radio.

On the air, live, Leslie helped lead me into it. "Matt, I know there are some things you want to talk about . . . ," and I said, "Yeah, I've been going through a rough time . . . ," and the show went on for four hours, me talking about it, taking calls, playing music—I remember playing "You Set the Scene" by Love.

For everyone who thinks that life is just a game
Do you like the part you're playing

It was an incredible relief, being able to talk about it openly, in prime radio-listening time in the biggest market in the country, maybe millions of people tuned in at any given moment. I shared my struggle the way I'd shared my love of music for decades. When it came time to come clean, I integrated it with music. There was an outpouring of love, people calling in wishing me luck or telling me about their own problems with alcohol and drugs, or about family members who were getting help. It was so moving.

While I was away, I'd call in to Leslie's show once in a while to check in with the audience. And when I got back to New York and went to the station for my first day back, there were people waiting for me in the lobby. One man said he'd been addicted to heroin and was hiding it from his wife and family and it was killing him, and how hearing me talk about it on the radio had made him decide to do something to get well. Look, I'm not going to pretend it's been easy all the time since getting out in '09. It's like skiing in a mine-field, and I've tripped up. But I have so much support. I may still be a work in progress, but I definitely have a clearer idea of the man I want to be.

I get asked all the time if rock is over, and I never know how to answer that one. Some people, like Gene Simmons, are absolutely convinced that it's been done for a while, and I don't see how anyone can deny that rock isn't driving the cultural conversation any longer. But I'm not prepared to write the eulogy for something that still has a beating pulse. Look at ticket sales for Rolling Stones stadium concerts. Or the packed bodies any given night for a local rock band at Bowery Ballroom. Or the visceral kick provided by a rampaging two-piece Brighton band, Royal Blood, who released their debut single "Out of the Black" in 2013. Are Florence and the Machine and Imagine Dragons something nonrock? What about Nathaniel Rateliff and the Night Sweats, and Twenty One Pilots? Jack White, Fall Out Boy, Dave Grohl?

I've stood onstage at Madison Square Garden and introduced Mumford and Sons to the roar of a sold-out crowd, had Kings of Leon help me celebrate my birthday in Ireland. I looked out at those seats filled with people a lot younger than I am, mostly, and I recognize them. I know what it's like to buy a ticket months in advance, to mentally mark the number of days until the concert, to feel your blood race when the lights go down, to hear the opening notes of the show and then take an exhilarating two-hour ride. Go ahead: try telling those people that rock is ancient history. For them, it's the present tense. It's being in the moment, sharing the same air with other fans and with those musicians up on the stage.

I think what people mean when they pronounce rock dead is that it doesn't have the same central place that it did whenever they discovered it, that at a certain point they stopped paying attention. Or maybe it's that elsewhere—in pop, R&B, EDM, country—boundary-stretching work is being done within a framework that's still vital and commercial, while alternative and mainstream rock feel comparatively stagnant. Are there rock singers and songwriters taking the kinds of creative leaps that Kendrick Lamar is? Are the modern equivalents of Springsteen and Petty fans listening to Americana/country artists like Jason Isbell or Kacey Musgraves? Is the Next Great Rock Band hiding in plain sight on Spotify, in the shadows because the means of exposure that once catapulted rock—like AOR, Active Rock and Alternative Radio, MTV—are making less of an impression on the mainstream, dwarfed by pop, urban, and country? Will it ever be possible again for a young artist, a rock version of Taylor Swift or Adele, to crash through the wall and fill stadiums with the sound of twenty-first-century rock music?

I can't live with rock being relegated to the past tense: I want to revisit the classic rock music I grew up with, but I need to be in the moment also. I want people born in this century to make, discover, and embrace rock music of their own and not just check in periodically to see what the heritage artists of the past are up to. It'd be great if more people heard Courtney Barnett or Royal Blood's music, and every time a band like Alabama Shakes causes a stir, it's a small victory.

There's a line in the rock 'n' roll film *American Hot Wax* where one character, a songwriter loosely based on Carole King, says, "I didn't have anything until I found the music," and that's how it was for me, and it still is. I think there are probably millions of kids who are finding their musical entry point now, possibly because they've heard of the Ramones or Led Zeppelin or Pearl Jam, or they're in the backseat of the family car when their dad is listening to a satellite classic rock station, and nothing has ever spoken to them as loudly and clearly as a song by Black Sabbath or Metallica. Once they're hooked, the possibilities for discovery are broader than they've ever been in our history, and maybe what they hear will lead them forward to the Black Keys and Eric Church or backwards to Buddy Holly and the New York Dolls. It's limitless now. And instant. What I do miss is the urgency of acquisition, the anticipation of bringing something home, opening the package, and slipping the record onto a stereo, or a CD into a player. The streaming services are great for the immediacy of discovery, finding something with one click. You can't slow down technology, and just because I come from an era where I had to save up dimes and quarters, get a ride to a record store, buy something, bring it back home, put it on a turntable, doesn't mean I got more out of that experience than someone who simply goes to Spotify and pokes around for a few seconds. There's always going to be a group of people—not all of them, not even a majority—who love and absorb music in a way that's like devotion. I guess the instant gratification means it's easier to get distracted; if you haven't made any kind of investment in time or money, it's much simpler to move along if something doesn't grab you in the first twenty seconds. When we brought home records, it was a ritual, a process, not a casual relationship with a keyboard where we can move on in a fraction of a second. We brought home albums from Korvettes and thought, I'm going to live with this for a while, read the liner notes and label copy, take it in. Because we wanted every record we bought to matter in some way, even if we didn't love every record equally.

It was so fulfilling to stoke your passion like that. But I

look at my fifteen-year-old daughter, the way she sits at the computer trying things out, making playlists, and there's a kind of beauty in that as well. I was one of those guys who embraced all new technology. When they came out with a dual CD burner, I was elated: I could make mixes like I would on cassette, but the quality was better. I would take those mixes and put them in little floppy-disc cases and number them, just put on all my favorite things, organized by era.

I made the biggest leap possible for a music fan, and I know exactly how fortunate I am to have been a witness and a participant in this world, to have traveled everywhere, met all of my heroes, spread the news about music that I thought mattered, to have been on stages and backstage with the biggest bands. I've screwed up enough times to know what a gift I've been given and how close I've come to squandering it. I think about every kid who watched the early Beatles singles spin around and around on plastic record players, devouring every note and wanting more. Their first US Capitol album was an invitation: *Meet the Beatles*, here they are, they belong to you and to everyone else buying this LP. I took that so seriously. Before I could read, I could look at the picture on the cover and I could listen. Over and over and over. What made me different, I guess, was that *that* was my world. It was all that mattered.

So many times I found myself in a situation that Matt Pinfield, the music-crazed kid analyzing every groove of a record album, would have found as far-fetched as becoming an astronaut or a Marvel superhero. In 2005, I was asked to host an international radio broadcast with the four core members of the Rolling Stones—Mick, Keith, Charlie, and Ron—to promote their new album (and, it turned out, the last studio album they've released as a band as of now), *A Bigger Bang*. Pinfield and the Stones. It was the first time they'd sat down and been interviewed together in decades, and I was the one who got to fire questions at them. And there was the time Leslie Fram and I, representing WRXP, were among the few people invited to London for the 9/9/09 launch of the Beatles Rock Band game and the release of their remastered catalog. Only three US radio stations got to participate. I'd been to Abbey Road once before, about five years earlier. I simply turned up at the door of the studio one day when I was in London for the Live 8 concert, introduced myself as an A&R guy from Columbia Records in New York City, and asked if I could take a look around. So I got a tour, and soaked up the sensation of being in the same space where pretty much every classic Beatles track was recorded. And I did the obligatory walk across the road from the album cover, because that's what all fans do when they visit.

For the Beatles Rock Band game launch, we got to stay at a cool hotel called the Gorge. As I looked around, I realized I was staying right next to the room where the photo for the inner sleeve of the Stones' *Beggars Banquet* was shot. I thought, I'm here for this big Beatles event, and my hotel is where Michael Joseph took that iconic Stones photo. It was insane rock synergy. I thought, There is something incredible going on here. The next day, we set up to do our radio show; we invited the Kooks to come in and sing a Beatles song, "You've Got to Hide Your Love Away," and did interviews with Giles Martin, the son of Beatles producer George Martin, and Tim Smith, who was EMI engineer Hurricane Smith's kid. We were there early and I took the opportunity to go into the control room, which I'd seen in so many old Beatles photographs, where George Martin would stand, smoking a cigarette, overseeing the Beatles' sessions. I tried to find the exact spot where he would have been, to get his visual perspective on the band and where each member of the Beatles would have set up to play, or do vocals. I needed to soak everything in, because if you care anything at all about rock music, its history and its importance, that room is sacred ground.

We got to see the original four-track machine that the band recorded *Sgt. Pepper* on. We walked through the room where they still keep the piano the Beatles used. It's there in the corner, the same fucking piano Paul played on songs like "Hey Jude." Everything about that room on Abbey Road is the way I'd always seen it in films and stills, the partitions, that weird mesh curtain. They left everything intact. Then Giles, who helped his dad with the remastering of all those tracks, walked in, came up to me, looked around, shook his head, and said, "Look at this shithole. You'd think they'd redecorate it." Maybe he was joking around, but I was shocked. "Giles, come on, man! Your dad's, my life, your life, everybody's life changed because of this room!" He just shrugged and said, "Yeah, I know, but they're keeping it the same." There are some people who aren't that senti- mental, I suppose, but for me, I wouldn't have wanted to see any renovations or "improvements." Some things you don't tamper with.

Music is a link to the past and a link to each other. It can be as solitary as a lonely kid in his room playing his favorite 45s until every note is scratched into his soul, or as com- munal as seventy thousand people at a stadium in Chicago saying farewell to the Grateful Dead. From the moment I got caught up in the excitement of rock, it was a calling in every sense. It reached out to me directly and drew me in, and I needed to absorb it, discover more about it, spread the word about it. When other parts of my life were crumbling, I could cling to this rock and it would save me. I can't imagine anyone having any more fun than I've had; I've accumulated a lifetime of music—some of it on worn-out vinyl, some of it stored on hard drives and MP3 players—and memories. I can't wait to hear the next new band, or walk into a club or concert hall and have my head blown back by someone I've never heard before. Music always finds new angles. It never stops. I chase that thrill, and then shout about it to everyone, as loudly as I can.

Acknowledgments

MATT WOULD LIKE TO THANK

Michelle Amible, Jose "Indian" and Denise Antao, Ian Astbury, Stu Bergen, Steve Blush, Will Botwin, John Boulos, Brian Bruden, Lexi and Dave Bryan, Michael Butscher, Tom Calderone, the Cascone Jacksonville family, Dan Catullo, Heather Cohen, Dominic and Kelly-Jane Cotter, Bart Dah, Chris and Walter Dallenbach, Carson Daly, Wade and Chachi Denes, Dean and Robert DiLeo, Michelle Dix, John Doelp, Dave Driewitz, John Easdale, Mark Felsot, Steve Flaks, Bill Flannagan, Leslie Fram, Tom Freston, Faye Gade, Cliff Galbraith, Patti Galluzzi, Frank Gibson, Geordie Gillespie, Charlene Goto, Alison Hagendorf, Shirley Halperin, Mike Henry, Stephen Hill, Kevin Horton, Miles Hunt, Matt Ianni, Jimmy Iovine, Andrew Keller, Steve Kingston, Joel Kleiman, Rick Krim, Lewis Largent, Tyler Lee, Steve Leeds, Dano Lehman, Cal Levine, Kurt Loder, Joe and Dave Machos, Judy Mallen, Clint Mansell, Mike Marrone, Rene Mata, Alexandra McAllister, Conor McAnally, Dermot McCormick, Judy McGrath, Greg McQuaid, Sean Patrick McShane, Mike McVey, Audrey Morrissey, Liz O'Donnell, Kevin Patrick, Tony Pelogrosi, Brian Phillips, Rich Phoenix, Pat Pierson, Matt Pollack, Ron Poore, Dan Redman, Robin Reinhardt, Suzanne Reynolds, the Riva Avenue EB Brotherhood (Robert Schweitzer, Rich O'Neill, Eric Hanson, Tim Clarke, and Billy Karmazan), Rich Robinson, Mik Rodriugez, Bill Royel, Pete Santiago, Robbie Schickner, Bryan Schock, Andy Schuon, Jay Shapiro, John Silva, Frank Sprock, Damien Starkey, Kurt Steffek, Ethan Stein, Marie Targos, Mike Tierney, Van Toffler, Thunderhead (Arthur, Jack, Laura, Don, and Joe), Scooter Ward, Eric Weiss, the Whiskey Vinyl/January Jane family (Pete Scialla, Rich McCary, Pat Via, Mitch Mitchell, Miguel, Cody, and Andre), Ed Wong, Ted Woods, and for everyone I forgot who had a major effect on my life, I apologize. This is it.

MITCHELL WOULD LIKE TO THANK

When I met Matt Pinfield, we connected immediately over the merits of Kinks B-sides, and which Tom Petty and the Heartbreakers album had the most perfect track sequencing. I never imagined that years later I'd be helping him put his knowledge and experiences down in book form, and for that opportunity—for getting me and Matt back in the same room—I have to thank Laura Nolan, who's been so supportive ever since I sent her a crazy, unsolicited book idea and she thought there might be some potential in it. Also thanks to John Glynn for steering this whole thing, and to Dan Cuddy and Elisa Rivlin for making sure we got things right. In that regard, Donna Cohen was immeasurably helpful and patient. Somewhere along this road, I met Gayle Lewis, and she listened, read, commented, calmed, and in general stuck by me and kept me sane. This book and my life wouldn't be what they are without her. And thanks, of course, to Matt for trusting me.